Fr Earl Willis

Who is Jesus?

1st Century Eyewitnesses Tell Their Stories

by

Cheryl Ann Wills

Lumen Christi Press

This book has been awarded the
Catholic Writers' Guild Seal of Approval

Genre: Scripture Meditation

Cover Photo: Head of Christ, Rembrandt, circa 1648

This book is dedicated to
Richard Bennett Foster III and Elaine S. Brancato Foster,
my parents and greatest cheerleaders.
They showed me how, when we allow Him,
God will do wondrous things in and through us.
I love you forever, Mom and Dad.

*May all the faithful departed,
through the mercy of God,
rest in peace.*

Thank you...

I am thankful to the Hard Bean Writers' Circle; we emboldened one another to write from our hearts again. I am also thankful to many friends around the country who took the time to read and give honest opinions of these stories, and to my Catholic Writers' Guild critique group for their critical encouragement. I thank Jean Ann Loughran, for giving her time to the final editing of this long-incubated work.

I give thanks to my three beautiful daughters who spurred me on to make a difference through my writing.

I give thanks to Ed, my husband of thirty-five years, for his brilliant and wise scripture translations throughout the book. My heart full of gratitude goes to him for constant support and belief in me.

Most of all, I thank God for the inspiration to imagine what could have been then, so that hearts may be touched for His purpose now.

Table of Contents

Before you turn the page, please read this:

The stories in this book are told by people who met Jesus in the Gospels. How is that possible? Several years ago I discovered Ignatian Imaginative Prayer. While I prayed and meditated, I put myself into a gospel passage, then journaled about what it felt like to be there, and what I might have said or done. Those first hours in imaginative prayer gave birth to <u>Who is Jesus? 1st Century Eyewitnesses Tell Their Stories</u>.

While reading, then, please keep in mind that the material is *based on* stories in the Bible. They have been developed, as I mentioned, through my application of imaginative prayer, as well as the meditation techniques called *Stillness*, developed by Ed Wills. The stories do not pretend to be Scripture, nor are they to be used as replacement of Scripture. Ed Wills translated all passages from their original text; some of those translations I paraphrased.

As historical fiction, the book intends to educate. I cross-referenced numerous books and reliable Internet sources on First Century Palestine culture to insure that, as much as possible, the stories accurately reflect that era's culture and historical context. I welcomed the gift of a trip to the Holy Land, which began the day after the first proof arrived in the mail, for it confirmed the authenticity of my work.

I am grateful to have learned more than I set out to discover and am fascinated by answers to many necessary questions. For instance:

> I was surprised that women and men were not separated in the local synagogues, and even that there were two types of synagogues in that particular pocket of history.

A farmer could realistically travel a distance after planting or before harvest; those seasons were not when I expected.

The Passover Seder was not for men only.

I had no idea that women owned successful businesses in 30 AD.

When the townsfolk heard the woman at the well headed their way because of the jingle of her anklets, we learn that is how a woman of her repute would have dressed.

I didn't realize that all centurions did not have to be Roman citizens. It was fun imagining where they may have come from.

Not only did people in Palestine eat different foods at different meals, they didn't eat what I would have thought. And, they rarely had a mid day meal.

Yes, the people of the era did use pillows.

Many personal and family names would appear in some cities but not in others. Sometimes names in one household were cross-cultural.

Young girls really were dedicated to the Lord, like Samuel, and lived in the Temple until their betrothal.

The days it took to walk from one place to another had to be considered in several stories.

The purpose of this book is to imagine what a First Century person who met Jesus might have thought and felt, and the impact that encounter may have produced. I hope each narrator's new understanding of who Jesus is will enhance your understanding of Him, too.

God bless you as you build your own story,

Cheryl Ann Wills

1 ♦ One Bright Night

Another knock. *Will they ever stop?* I listened from the back room where I slept with my younger sisters. Father sighed wearily as he rose to open the door.

For weeks since King Herod called the census, our town overflowed with excitement. It meant a lot of money for the innkeepers. It also meant that too many unhappy strangers crowded the streets. Being forced to travel from far away with little notice made them miserable. Their irritable moods increased as scarcity of food, water, and shelter also increased.

"No room at this house," I heard Father's annoyance and then strained to hear the response. *It's probably not the usual traveler because he didn't slam the door.* I tiptoed past my gently snoring siblings and peeked around the curtain - the wall of our room.

"I'm sorry." Father actually sounded apologetic. "I wish I could help. We're over-crowded as it is." A pause. "I know, I know," he continued in an almost gentle voice. "What else can I do?" He raised his arms in that way when he doesn't have answers.

I heard a woman plead.

"I have only one spot where you can find rest. It's not a pleasant offering. So, please, don't be offended. It's the cave where I shelter my few livestock."

What is father thinking? Offering our cave to people? I snuck up behind him and peered around to look at the person he thought might want to rest there. *Such a kind face on this man, despite his haggard look.* Behind him, a donkey carried his wife. *Her eyes are gentle, too.* A heavy shawl covered her cloak to protect her from the cool night air. *More people on a long and tiring trip.* I stared at them more closely. *I'm practically a child myself but even I can tell her baby will be born very soon!* And then I approached my father with no invitation – the unthinkable.

"Father, surely they can stay here! I'll give up my mat for the woman."

"Child!" I had startled him. "What are you doing here, eavesdropping? Go back to your room, Sarah, which is not your room alone. Did you consider that when you offered your mat? Now, go!"

I slunk back to my room and heard the man say, "It will have to do. No." He hesitated. "I mean, thank you. We are very grateful."

Father gathered his cloak and a lantern. Then the door closed behind him.

Visions of guests sleeping with the animals haunted me. *I'll wake up at dawn. Maybe then I can help them get comfortable.* After what seemed hours, I succumbed to a fitful sleep. I never heard my father come home.

I don't know how long I slept before I sensed movement outside. My eyes popped open. *It's not dawn. What's happening?* Even Mother wasn't up yet to begin the cooking fire for our boarders and us. I lay perfectly motionless and strained to figure out the unusual sounds. *Many feet are shuffling. But not just the feet of men. That's the clip-clop of animal hooves!* Once more, I tiptoed past my sisters to our curtain. The outer room was empty. I stole to the door and, ever so quietly, cracked it open.

What, in the name of all that is good, am I seeing? Shepherds and their herds scuffed down our narrow street. With bright eyes and animated faces they chattered noisily. I risked opening the door all

4

the way and stepped onto the threshold. *What? They're going to our cave!*

I have to do something. But, what? I closed the door and cautiously moved to my sleeping parents. *I am just about to break another rule.* We were never to enter their sleeping place unless our lives were threatened. My head spun with options and thoughts of consequences. *This is serious. Waking them is better than leaving the house alone at night.*

I crept to Mother's side, and whispered in her ear, "Mother?"

"What? What is it, Sarah?" Her eyes sprung open. *Ooh! She woke up faster than I expected.*

"Mother, there are a lot of shepherds and animals outside. They're all headed to our cave."

She blinked to adjust to the light that shone through our tiny window. She shifted slightly to focus on the sounds outside. "Benjamin," she spoke softly and touched Father's shoulder. No one wants to make him angry by waking him before dawn.

"Hmm?" He barely stirred.

"Benjamin. There are people outside. Something's wrong."

In one swift motion, my ever-protective father rose to his feet and threw on a coat. In a flash he was at the door and flung it open. He raised his arm to shade his eyes, squinting to make out the moving shapes in the street. *Where is that light coming from?*

"Ruth! Quickly. Come here," he called in a hoarse whisper.

Her robe already on, Mother scampered in response to his urgency. Naturally, I ran up, too. We gasped. *What's going on?* Shepherds and their sheep crammed the street.

"You stay here," my father ordered both of us. "I will investigate."

"Oh, Father, please can I go with you? Surely this is something we'll never see again."

My mother nodded slightly and peered at him with those eyes that said, yes.

I hastily threw on my cloak and covered my head. We pushed into the smelly crowd that carried us to our livestock. A twinkly brightness illuminated everything and everyone. People and animals pressed together and moved in one great swell. The oddity of walking shoulder to shoulder with shepherds didn't seem to matter.

The closer we got to our destination, the less we all spoke. Even the animals hushed.

That light is coming from one great star. My heart pounded as my feet hurried to keep up with the shepherds.

Suddenly, like they all sensed the same sound from far away, the animals halted. Naturally, everyone followed their lead and stood in silence, too. Father and I were at the back so we wended our way forward. Beginning at the front, people knelt. Some bowed their heads. A kneeling wave rolled back through the crowd. *Such strange behavior of men and animals.* Crazy thoughts spun through my head as I tried to make sense of it all.

And then we reached the entrance to the cave. *Oh!* My breath caught. Without discussion, Father and I dropped to our knees. The sight was beyond my imagination.

In our manger filled with fresh straw, lay a tiny boy baby in white swaddling cloths. His newborn eyes were tightly shut. By his side, nestled in piles of hay, lounged the young woman I saw on the donkey. She wore a faint smile. Her serious eyes reflected both weariness and compassion. A tall man with eyes that sparkled though half closed from exhaustion, stood near mother and child. *Yes, that's the man at our door last night.* Love and pride shone through his smile. And relief.

I looked up. The light from that great star seemed to shine up from the family at the same time. *This is no ordinary family.*

Tears trickled down my face. My even breath revealed a sense of contentment in my heart. I glanced at my father. On a face relaxed with peace, he allowed tears to stream freely. He turned his face to me, stared into my eyes, and smiled. My father is a good man, but he rarely smiled. And I always knew he was my protector, but he never put his arm about my shoulder like he did that night. *Father is different.* A new sense of security sprouted in my heart.

Is this a dream? I closed my eyes. When I opened them again, the scene remained. I will close my eyes now and make sure the picture of this night stays with me forever. *A change in me has already begun. I want to always remember the exact feeling of its start.*

I'm thankful I took the chance to wake my parents because the night was truly like no other. That night changed my family, my friends, and me. It changed the world. Forever.

Based on the story in Luke 2:1-20

2 ✦ Our God Is Faithful

Please bear with me as I tell my story. I want everyone to understand that I'm not just some crazy old woman.

Everyone delighted in Mary. Giving, loving and forgiving describe her. To teach a child like her was a pleasure. She eagerly learned things of the spirit as well as the ways of everyday living, which many call mundane. Mary's aged father died before her sixth birthday and her gentle mother not many years later. Though sad for her heartache, I thrilled to step in to meet a young girl's needs. We were as close as a mother and child, a sweet gift to a childless widow like me. As she neared womanhood, her graceful countenance reminded me of a gazelle – swift in purpose, full of poise. The women who lived with us in the Temple often commented about how happy Mary would make her future husband. But I knew something the other women did not.

"Anna," Mary confided one afternoon as we sewed vestments. "You were there when my parents presented me to God. Do you remember?"

The scene flashed through my mind. I smiled, "Oh, yes, child."

"And I took a vow of virginity."

"Yes," I replied, curious as to where the conversation would go.

"Anna," she nearly pleaded, "my vow was for life. I never intend to take a husband."

The linen dropped from my hands. I looked intently into her midnight blue eyes that allowed her soul to emerge, eyes that now glistened. *She is definitely sincere. But I know the rules. She stays here until her womanhood when the priest chooses her betrothed.* I opened my mouth to remind her but, to my utter amazement, I said, "Yes, Mary. And you will remain a virgin. I don't know how but something in me believes God will intervene on your behalf. Your vow will not be broken." Salty streams traveled down the crevices of my time worn face.

Mary lowered her head. We picked up our sewing and remained silent.

All of Israel knows the Holy of Holies can only be entered by the High Priest. In fact, he enters only on the Day of Atonement. Was it her spiritual devotion combined with her unusual demeanor that led the High Priest to disregard that law? Or did an angel direct him?

Late into one evening I prayed in the Court of Women, and heard the priest enter the Inner Court. I'm certain I did not dream this, even though my eyes fluttered open. He was not alone. My Mary, as I called her, stepped softly as the deer behind him, wearing a veil over her bowed head. I lowered my eyes, then peeked to see them both kneel before the Altar of Sacrifice. I threw my hand over my mouth when, with not a word spoken between them, they arose, moved up the steps and past the Altar of Incense, and through the Holy Place. He lifted the Veil and they entered the Holy of Holies. Instantly I shut my eyes and began to pray. *I hope they don't hear my pounding heart and realize they're not alone.*

I'm thankful that the spirit of God led me into the secret place in my heart, where I have no awareness of time or space, the place that is nothing of me and everything of God. I wanted to think of nothing, not what my imagination might lead me to.

A slight movement below caused me to stir just in time to witness a radiant child exit the Holy of Holies. Instinctively, I lowered my head out of respect. Even as my heart questioned what I saw, I sensed that one day God would reveal the meaning of the event. From that day forward, Mary and I spent more hours than usual in prayer and fasting. Though we never spoke a word of that night, I think she knew I knew.

The time when Mary reached the age of maturity came too soon for me. According to the Law of Moses, she should return to her parents' house or to her betrothed. Her parents, as I mentioned, were deceased. The day approached for the choosing of her betrothed by the chief priest. She rushed into my quarters one afternoon, her face flushed with color and her brows deeply furrowed.

"Mary! What's wrong, my child?"

She slid to the floor and placed her head on my lap, "This cannot be." She tried to suppress a loud sob.

I closed my eyes as I smoothed her hair away from her face. *Oh, God give me insight.* "Mary, try not to be afraid. You were chosen by God to remain pure. We must rest in Him." She sat by me long into the evening. Neither of us spoke again that night.

The next day, before dawn, we met for prayer. It was the eighth day of our fast and the day a betrothed would be chosen. Several young men and their families had bathed outside the Huldah Gate and waited in the Plaza.

We watched from the Court of Women. The entire process of choosing a betrothed I had not witnessed in all my years and to this day have not seen again. One by one, men were disqualified. The priest called all remaining eligible men to meet in the council chamber. Each man dragged himself with head hung low, shoulders drooped, and no smile.

Though our fast could be broken the next morning Mary and I chose to keep it. Three days later the applicants returned. I glanced at Mary as we entered the court at about the same time as the men. I marveled. *She is perfectly serene.* The applicants each carried a fresh lily stalk, which they handed the priest. The priest took the stalks into the sanctuary.

After what seemed hours, the priest exited the sanctuary and handed each stalk to its owner. Spots appeared on each stalk.

Except one. Only the stalk that belonged to Joseph remained fresh and unblemished, its bloom fresh and full. To the priest it meant that Joseph, the carpenter, was the chosen spouse.

Some people present thought the test wasn't good enough, which provoked the priest. He demanded a dove be brought to him. And then he called for Mary. With her head held low, and without a hint of anxiety, she glided down the steps to the feet of the priest where she then knelt.

"Rise," he gently commanded. "Now, take this dove. Walk into the center of the candidates, and when you reach them, let it fly freely."

As she carried the white bird to the waiting candidates, the priest spoke loudly, "Watch this, you false interpreters of the sign of God! This creature – pure and innocent - cannot hear our discussion. It lives in the will of the Lord. It only understands the language of God. Hold your stalks high! Once this maiden frees the dove, it will settle on a stalk and then on the head of the man who owns it. The man it settles on shall take Mary."

At the priest's direction, Mary released the dove. It settled on Joseph's head.

Joseph was visibly shaken. He voiced his fear at taking in a maiden since he was an older man with four grown sons.

But after praying, the priest pronounced that God had made the choice. And he blessed Joseph saying, "Joseph, the Lord has found you just. And, so, He chose you. Go in peace and let it be."

My mind swirled with wild thoughts. My heart beat like wings of a bird chased by his predator. But when I met Mary to help gather her things to leave, she took my hand and whispered, "God has fulfilled His Word."

And though I didn't understand, a sense of perfect contentment washed over me. Still, a great sadness to let her go found its way into my heart.

For two years not a day passed without a prayer for Mary and her betrothed. *Had they consummated their marriage? According to Mary's confirmation, impossible!*

One day I awoke with a quickening in my spirit. I hurried to prayer, elated to see ancient Simeon at Temple that day. His presence here since the days in Alexandria, when he worked on the translation of Holy Scripture to Greek, confirmed the hope of wondrous things in store for us all. After all, when an angel speaks, it is surely Truth. It was easy for me to believe God kept Simeon on this earth for three hundred years in order that the angelic words would come to pass. But I often wondered if I would have the chance to rejoice with him. At eighty-four, my aching bones were ready for a final rest.

Around the fifth hour, word spread that a first-born male would be presented to the Lord. I hurried to the court inside Huldah Gate in search of the joyful occasion. It's wonderful to witness the presentation of a boy baby. I followed Simeon through the throngs of people and nearly fainted when we reached them. *This baby's mother is my Mary. No! God promised!*

While my mind raced to untangle memories and promises, old Simeon whisked the child from Mary. He raised the baby toward heaven and pronounced, "O God, my King, now you have released your servant so that I may depart in peace as you promised. Because my eyes have seen your Salvation, whose appearance you have long prepared so that all the world will see. He is the glory of your people, Israel, and the Light who will reveal the hidden ways of God to the nations."

I fell to my knees and clasped my hands. My heart told me his words were Truth.

The child's parents looked at Simeon wide-eyed. He faced my Mary, "I tell you, this infant shall fall into the depths and rise again, and this sign will cause great division among many in Israel. It will be like a sword slicing into your own soul, as well. And the thoughts of hearts will be revealed." Simeon carefully set the child into his father's arms and bowed his head.

I stood up and inched my way to the family. I squeezed past the whisperers who wondered about the old man's words. At her side, I spoke softly, "Mary." She pivoted at the sound of my voice and threw herself into my frail arms. After a few moments, I pulled back and peered into her calm and gentle eyes. *Her vow has been kept.* Tears spilled down my cheeks. I twisted away then, to meet the eyes of her quiet infant and smiled. *He knows me. I'm certain.*

I raised my arms to heaven. I rejoiced and gave thanks to the Lord who is good. And I spoke the words of the Prophet Isaiah, "The Lord will give you a miraculous sign. A virgin will give birth to a son. She will proclaim him Emmanuel. Emmanuel – God is among us." *Do you hear me, people?*

From that day, I continue to proclaim with newfound energy to all who choose to hear: The redemption of Jerusalem, and of all peoples, is at hand!

Based on the story in Luke 2:22-38

3 ✦ A Memorable
First Meeting

What's going on? Raised voices interrupted my thoughts as I entered our tent to rest after our first meal. I threw on my cloak. I held it close as I stepped outside again; even though the sun was full, I shivered in the morning chill. I followed the noise to the outer edge of our camp.

The men huddled around someone, engrossed in conversation. The women gathered around a young woman on a donkey. Her arms wrapped tightly around a baby as her tired eyes darted back and forth across the land and at us. *The fear in those eyes tells me she hopes she won't find what she's looking for.*

I approached the men's group. *I'll learn more from them than the women.* They were too fascinated to bother with a woman listening in.

"We're traveling to Egypt." The stranger released a heavy sigh as he rubbed the back of his neck.

"Egypt!" the incredulous reply from several at once.

"What part of Egypt? You could have quite a distance yet."

"Why would you take your wife and baby to Egypt? And, why did you risk travel alone through the night?"

"Who are you?"

The man straightened himself to answer, "I am Joseph, of the House of David."

Confused and alarmed that a Jew would stop at our camp, the men rattled off more questions about why the journey.

"I. Well. It's," the tired, halted response. "I sensed the need to leave Bethlehem in haste, to protect my son."

"You came all the way from Bethlehem?"

"Come. Eat. Rest. We will water your donkey."

Didn't anyone else hear him say he had to protect his son? Whatever could they have done that leaving Bethlehem would protect their child? Not only is that unusual, but these strangers are Jews. Our ancestors are related, true. But, we've had few, if any, dealings with Jews for over a hundred years. They must be desperate for companionship.

"Hurry, Photina!" The women in our caravan waved me over. As they helped the young mother and child settle close to the fire, they buzzed like a swarm of honeybees.

When the woman sat down, her body seemed to relax even while she still clasped the baby close. The tension in her eyes remained. *Such a pretty and young mother. It's too bad she's obviously filled with so much anguish.*

Though the fear remained, her eyes looked with kindness upon everyone around her. She told us her name was Mary, but didn't share more information. She nodded thanks for a drink of water, a piece of bread and a handful of olives. The tightness in her face softened as she unwrapped her little boy and allowed his head to lean against her.

Look at us. Not one can keep our eyes off that child's soft face. It's not that he was more beautiful than any other mother's child, though he was one that even other mothers exclaimed over. It seemed like he drew us to him; somehow he kept our faces riveted on his.

His mother looked at us, and at him, and at us again. *Her smile reveals a secret.*

After the initial moments of astonishment at our own reaction, the whispering hum resumed. "Who is this child?"

"What does his mother know that we do not?"

"Why is it so hard to take our eyes from him?"

I glanced over at the boy's father. He sat and ate near the men's fire, with eyes that struggled to stay open, even while they kept constant sight of his family.

Caring and gentle. Perhaps because he's so much older than his wife, he understands life and its dangers. What a lucky woman and child, regardless of his age.

Soon the baby cried. The visitors had nothing to make a shelter. *They did leave in a hurry.*

"Come to my tent, it's the emptiest. You can meet your baby's needs and rest in private," I invited. I knew Benjamin, my husband at the time, would be occupied in the camp until nightfall.

Mary stood up and looked at her husband. When he nodded, she thanked and followed me. Inside the tent, I directed her to where I slept. I shook out my goat skin pillow and said, "Rest here with your child. Meet his hunger in peace."

She smiled. "Thank you, Photina." The grateful mother adjusted herself on the mat and leaned into the pillow with a soft sigh.

I stepped outside as she wrapped her cloak around her and her child, took him to her breast, and quieted his tears of hunger. *A suckling infant delivers a sense of peace - even if the child is not my own.*

Hours later, Mary lifted the door of my tent to enter the noon sunlight. Her rest revealed more beauty. The difference in her from my friends and myself is profound. Even though she's young, she seems to embody both tremendous wisdom and sweet innocence.

After several days' travel we needed more time to replenish our energy, as well as that of our animals. Our caravan leader decided to stay in camp another night. He invited the foreigners to spend the night with us and even continue to this side of Mt. Karkom, our destination. I learned that the child's father gratefully accepted the offer in return for his help with our flocks.

Before sunset, a great sadness swept through the camp. Another caravan stopped to set up camp nearby. King Herod lost his mind once more. Tears splashed every face as they described how his troops advanced through the little town of Bethlehem and the outlying region and killed every male child under the age of two years. The story went that he feared rumors of a king of Jews born there. He wanted to make certain no child in the region would survive to take power from him one day. The wailing from homes and streets of the towns and villages in Judea filled the air to the heavens. Though it had been such a long time since the Samaritans and Jews lived as friends, we never wished such a tragedy on them. Our wails joined theirs.

With ashen faces Joseph and Mary ran to each other. Joseph gathered his family into his strong arms. Their bodies shook together as floods of tears spilled. I recalled the words of Joseph, "I sensed the need to leave Bethlehem to protect my son." *How did he know?*

I reflected on my life. Benjamin would never comfort me like that, even in a situation like this.

Heavy hearts accompanied us throughout the next day's journey. Thoughts of the massacre tumbled through everyone's minds like fierce river rapids. Not one of us could imagine such a horrific experience. *This is the first time I've ever been thankful to have no children. I don't want to re-live that anguish as a mother.*

After several days some of the sorrow in the camp lifted and we even laughed at our children's antics. Thanks be to God for the innocence of children; they were oblivious to their good fortune. The journey to our new settlement continued with a spirit of gratitude.

"Oh, let me help you," Joseph or Mary would always speak up. The newcomers were soon no longer strangers. It was easy to welcome people whose dispositions were as sweet as their baby.

At last we arrived at our new home. The first night we camped together. The area would be divided among the families the next day when we could build permanent housing. That night we celebrated our safe arrival around fires where we shared food, stories, and song.

As dawn greeted us, the women set out to collect firewood and water. Mary and Joseph loaded their donkey to continue to Egypt.

"Mary!" I called as I set down my water jug and ran to say good-bye. With her little boy wrapped close to her, she turned to me. Her soft, dark eyes locked on mine. "I wish you well on your journey. I wish you safety and provision."

She replied in her quiet voice, "Thank you. And so with you." Her warm embrace was like a protective covering over me. *She is a true nurturer.*

I hesitated before I asked, "May I take one more look at the child?"

"Of course, Photina." She lifted the cloth that protected his face from sand that swirled around us.

"Tell me his name again?"

"His name is Jesus."

I peered again into his eyes. *Deep, clear, bottomless wells.* Those wells glimmered joy that my heart longed for. I leaned and placed my lips on his forehead. *This is a seal for us to meet again.* Little did I know that many years later, back in Samaria, Mary's secret would be revealed and my life would change forever.

Based on the story in Matthew 2:13-18

4 ♦ Joy In Finding Him

Our town of Nazareth is tiny, which means we're all involved in each other's lives. Maybe that's why Jesus and I were so close. Or, maybe it's because my father was an artisan like Joseph, his father. Our mothers enjoyed trips to the well together and hours carding and spinning side by side. Though cousins, we considered ourselves brothers.

We did everything together – from playing as youngsters to studying at synagogue, from helping our mothers as children, to apprenticeships with our fathers. We were inseparable. It wasn't until a certain event occurred that made me step back and see him in a different light that I understood how different we actually were.

It was the year we were both 12; according to the Law and tradition, we were nearly men. We traveled with many families to Jerusalem for the Passover Feast. We no longer ran and played on the caravan like when we were children. Still, we walked back and forth and visited with all the families. It was a good way to separate myself from my younger siblings and cousins.

Jerusalem energized me every time I visited. To take part in the Feast of the Passover increased my excitement. The noisy bustle of busy people gathered together for one purpose - many of them pilgrims dressed in the colors of their homeland, singing psalms as they moved through the narrow streets - the bleating of unblemished animals sold and prepared, the calling of vendors, and the occasional triple blast of seven silver trumpets from the men's court to call the pious, combined to make me more aware that I am part of something greater than little Nazareth. So many, from so far away, gathered in one city to celebrate the one God.

When we arrived, the families in our caravan scattered to the homes of friends or relatives; some of them to rooms they rented. Days later, when it was time for the return journey, exhausted from the festival, we all looked forward to home.

I was so tired I decided to stay with my family on the journey rather than wander with Jesus. As always, parents never worried about the whereabouts of their children; everyone was safe with one neighbor or another. And that's how the crisis arose.

When we stopped the first night, Joseph, with a pale faced twisted in agony, approached my father. My father's eyebrows knit together as he shook his head in response to whatever Joseph asked.

"What's wrong, Father?" I ran up as Joseph took off for the next family group.

"No one seems to know where Jesus is. When did you last see him?"

"Well, now that you ask me, Father, I don't think I've seen him all day." *Where is Jesus?* A dark veil covered my heart.

I started running to all of the cousins who traveled with us. "Have you seen him? Have you seen Jesus?"

No one had seen him all day. I found Mary. Her face was ashen. She took my hands in both of hers and looked at me with wet and questioning eyes. Her hands shook and her lower lip quivered. She didn't need to speak. Mary had always been like a mother to me; I knew her thoughts.

"We'll find him, Mary," I whispered. I choked back tears and hoped my hoarse voice sounded courageous. She slowly nodded her head in agreement while tears trickled down her face.

When Joseph returned from searching, he and Mary decided to return to Jerusalem at dawn to find my friend. I asked if I could join them and, when they agreed, I raced to ask my parents' permission.

"Of course, you'll go!" my father boomed. "He is your brother!"

Mother woke me at dawn. She sent me on my way with a flask with of water mixed with a little wine, and a bag with figs, olives, and flat bread.

We pushed the donkey a bit harder than on the way out as this was not a leisurely family excursion. Before dusk we arrived back at the home of Joseph's relatives where they had stayed during the feast. No one had seen Jesus.

We rubbed our sore and aching feet with oils, then refreshed ourselves with food and drink. In a short while, several men, myself included I will add, visited a few more of the homes where our party had stayed during the feast. We returned late - drained and disheartened. The city seemed bigger than ever.

The next morning, everyone – relatives, neighbors, Mary, Joseph and I – ate earlier than usual and headed out. There was no time to waste.

Someone told us they saw him at the market, buying bread and olives for what looked like a group of street urchins. His parents stared at each other at this news, which made twinkles of hope kindle in their eyes.

The three of us rushed to the Lower City. Without the task at hand, I would have loved another trip to that marketplace. Jerusalem's market is so much bigger than ours, even bigger than the one in beautiful Sepphoris. Booths were crammed together around the outside edges. Vendors sat under canopies or stood at the front of booths with their wares spread before them. Each one tried to call louder than his competitor. "Look here!" Or, "My prices are lowest!" And, "I have the best!"

Everything anyone could want or need lined the marketplace, which had been built up and down the city steps - from colorful fabric to sturdy pots, to fresh vegetables and lowing animals. The strong aroma of sheep and goats was life-giving to me. It represented food for all. Of course, it didn't mean food for all. That's why they saw Jesus buying for the poor.

We each covered a section of the market. We described to each vendor, in minute detail, the kind and serious-looking 12 year old boy we looked for. Most stared back with no expression. After all, hundreds of people of all sizes and ages passed by every day. A few said, yes, they had seen someone who might be him but, of course, they had no idea of his whereabouts now. Others laughed at our absurdity to think they could remember one face among hundreds.

Hours later, the search party re-grouped at a designated crossroads. As we approached, the group whispered to one another. *No one is smiling.*

Then one of the brothers ran up and caught his breath before he announced, "I met a woman who said someone who might have been him had begged alms from her. He said he would use them to buy herbs and figs to help physicians care for the sick." Smiles broke out, heads nodded, and voices lifted in hope. We rushed as one body in search of local physicians.

The growing anguish on Joseph's face, evidenced by a continual drain of color, was unbearable to witness as we met one after another who confirmed the report, always with a similar story, "Yes, a boy meeting his description shadowed me from house to house for quite a while. He seemed to have everything I recommended to heal the sick. My patients were grateful to be able to make the poultices and teas immediately because of him. No, I have no idea where he is now."

Finally, the sun began to set once more. Joseph's eyes brimmed. Mary, being her positive self again, took his hand, looked straight into his face and said, "Keep hope." Without another word, we headed to our host's home.

Mary, Joseph and I picked at the food prepared for us, spoke little, and retired soon after.

The next morning, as pink waves of light began their dance on the buildings around us, we three ate our breakfast of goat's milk and bread dipped in herbs and olive oil. We didn't look at each other or speak.

Mary broke the silence, "As I prayed through the night, I became convinced that we will find Jesus at the Temple." *There's that little spark of light in Joseph's eyes again.*

Instead of lingering to finish our meal, our host packed olives and figs for us, and a few fresh flasks so that we could hurry to the Temple, even before the other searchers arrived.

By the time we left it was the third hour. Already, people jammed the streets. The Royal Porch was flooded with people, too. We wove our way through them to the great hall off Solomon's Porch, and there he was. About twenty teachers gathered around him. Most wore looks of wide-eyed astonishment, while the eyes of some squinted in anger.

We inched closer and listened. They asked him questions about Scripture. They murmured and looked at each other every time he replied with confidence, though not boasting. Some were surprised and nodded in agreement. Others were embarrassed and annoyed and said things like, "How can he possibly know this?

We have studied our entire lives. How can he understand more than we do?"

As soon as the questions ceased for a moment, with respect and boldness combined, Mary stepped her way through the men to her son. When she touched his shoulder and he looked up at her, it was the first time he had seen her at the crowded porch.

"Son, why did you do this to us? Your father and I have been worried sick looking for you." Tears squeezed out the corners of her midnight-blue eyes.

Jesus' eyes flashed confusion as he scanned the hall to find Joseph and me.

He turned back to face his mother. "Why were you searching for me? Didn't you know that I had work to do in my Father's house?"
Dead silence. No one moved a muscle.

Now I'm confused. Whose house? Joseph is his father. They live in Nazareth. I looked up at Joseph. His soft gaze remained on Jesus while silent tears escaped.

Jesus stood up, bowed respectfully to the elders, and followed Mary to Joseph who hugged him. He looked right at me. I half smiled, still in a state of wonder.

"I'm so thankful we found you." I couldn't sputter any other words, though they didn't match the joy in me that was like none I had ever known. Even to this day, the joy in that moment when we found Jesus has no comparison.

He nodded. The four of us headed back to the home of their relatives. No one said a word.

I didn't sleep well for weeks after that event. No one in Nazareth spoke about it in public, though I'm certain everyone was aware of what had happened.

My friendship with Jesus continued to flourish. We both became hard working artisans, I a baker, him a carpenter. I married. He did not.

By the time we were both 30 years old, he began to teach all over Galilee and Judea. It was obvious to me that my best friend was more than just a great man.

Long before he was betrayed and hung on a cross to die, I discovered what he meant about being in his Father's house that day when we were nearly men. And the best decision my wife and I ever made was to follow him to the end, which was actually the beginning.

Based on the story in Luke 2:41-51

5 ✦ We Were Different - Now I Know Why

Jesus and I grew up together in Nazareth. But he was different from all of my friends and me.

Here's an example. We used to race to prove who ran the fastest. One day I tripped one of the kids I competed against. Typical for me, I narrowed my eyes at the guy and yelled, "Look out, will you?" like it was his fault. I picked up my pace and left him there, even though his leg and arm were badly scraped up. What do you think happened next? Jesus held up his hand to stop the race and walked over to the boy. He actually took the hem of his own cloak and wiped the dust and blood from the boy's leg and forearm. He stretched out a hand to help the boy stand and asked, "Better?" Micah smiled huge and bobbed his head. My friends wore looks that reflected my thoughts: *it's like we're watching snow fall in summer*.

And another example was when we began classes at the synagogue. He always learned the material super fast and went ahead in the studies. Not only that, sometimes it seemed like he knew more than our rabbi.

I liked him enough. But sometimes I didn't hang out with him because - well - it was more fun to live on that narrow line between good and bad. Jesus seemed planted on the good side.

Jesus' father, Joseph, was a carpenter. My father was a farmer. Because everyone held them in high regard, my family didn't look down on his, as often happens between farmers and artisans. His family was hard-working, honest, and giving. Still, our families didn't do much together. I think it was because our routines didn't coincide. Except on the Sabbath.

Everyone, artisans and farmers alike, gathered on Sabbath. And that's when Jesus shone. When he was old enough to read the scroll in synagogue, we all looked hypnotized. There was something about his voice, and the way he read, that made us think he wanted us to grasp some kind of hidden meaning.

We all grew up and started our own families. Except Jesus. He spent so much time learning and teaching, I guess he couldn't fit in a family.

I had a nice plot of land that my father gave me. My olive and fig groves flourished under my excellent care. After all, my father trained me. I found ready buyers everyday at the Sepphoris market – almost four miles from Nazareth - because my fruits, oils, and pastes were beautiful and their aroma called to people.

To say life was hard is an understatement. We had to pay the imperial taxes on top of our own temple tax, plus our tithes. All those taxes made it impossible to thoroughly enjoy the fruit of our own labor. Yes, I had a plot of land, but my wife and children and I lived with my parents and four of my siblings in a small, two-room house. Why? Because no one could make a profit, no matter how good their product. But it was more than not being able to get ahead; we could barely keep our heads above water. Each household had to constantly borrow to buy seed. Then we'd pray we wouldn't need to sell ourselves into slavery to pay those debts. Who could ransom us if we did that?

We had no choice but to sell to the Romans in Sepphoris. Not only was the market huge and accommodating, the population was many times greater than little Nazareth. Sepphoris was one of the beautiful cities built by Herod and he considered this one his pride and joy. I tried to avoid the taxes that he forced on us, but collectors always found me. It was easy for them to keep track of us. Whenever we were at market, Herod's spies, as we called them, kept close tabs on us.

Many of us chose to cheat – even our own neighbors - just to feed our children. It was simple to fool young shoppers with how much

I placed on the scale, because they talked nonstop to their friends and didn't pay attention to what they did. It was easier to cheat the old folks. They could be distracted in noisy crowds just like children, so I could place my hand on the scale or toss in a small stone with no one's notice. Did I feel guilty? Sometimes. Like when I cheated poor old widows. Still, I didn't feel guilty enough to change my ways. I needed every drachma I could scrape up. Besides, we never knew when the next tax hike would hit us.

My greatest embarrassment is forever chiseled in my memory. As usual, the men stood around the courtyard to talk after services one day. The women had hurried home to set out the late afternoon meal of Shabbat - what we call our religious observance of rest on the Sabbath. Jesus still lived in Nazareth then. Our typical conversation trailed from the weather to crops to taxes and, finally, the Roman occupation.

"I'm done with these Romans," I spat on the ground. "They cheat us, they accuse us falsely, and they make life miserable. Where is our redeemer?" "Yes," Joel chimed in, shaking his raised fist in the air. "We need to be rescued, and the Romans need to be annihilated." Agreement rumbled through the small group. "Where is Elijah? Aren't we oppressed enough?" I moaned. "Isn't it time?" We all lamented with flushed faces and voices that grew louder.

"Men," Jesus spoke in that quiet voice of his that demanded attention. "I agree life is unbearably hard. But perhaps before we blame all of our hardships on the Romans, we should consider our own actions. What does our own law call for?"

As one, we hung our heads.

"Do we forgive each other debts as we would hope they would ours?"

I began to feel exposed – like he knew my bad secret and was telling the world.

He didn't stop there. "And, yes, they cheat us and steal from us. But which one of us can claim perfect integrity? Perhaps we should change our own ways first."

And, no kidding, he looked directly into my eyes. *How did he know?* A well of sadness rose up within me.

You would think after that admonition, almost a warning, I would immediately mend my ways. But not one week later when I entered Sepphoris, a tax collector called to me for all to hear. "Justus, you seem to have forgotten to pay your tax the last time you sold here."

Traitor, I mumbled under my breath. Then, out loud, "Oh. I'm. Well, I meant to," I stumbled. *Trapped again.*

"Let's see what you plan to sell today."

He rummaged through my cart and stole a handful of figs for his own belt. He miscounted – in his favor of course – everything I had with me. "Today you will pay one shekel."

"But – but - but. I can't sell enough to pay such a tax."

"You should have thought of that earlier."

I sighed and scuffed away with knit brows and pursed lips. Then I hoped that yet another friend could lend me money. My anger refueled. I continued doing business as usual.

As we trudged through life, we clung to the hope that soon Elijah would herald the arrival of our redeemer.

After more than ten years of marriage, my family of seven still lived crammed into my father's house. Miscounted purchases here and weighted scales there continued. Every day I tried to sneak past the tax collector. I rarely succeeded. I considered myself a poor provider. I was tired. And angry. "How long, O Lord? How long?" I cried out each night.

One night, I could barely hold my head up as I dragged my empty cart toward home, with a nearly empty belt tied to my waist. My equally tired and angry neighbors chatted. Judah mentioned a rumor about a man named John. He preached about repentance and said things like, "Get everything ready for the coming of the Lord," and, "Someone is coming after me who is much greater than me. Compared to him I am less than a slave. I am not even worthy to take off his sandals."

My breath caught. *What?* I stopped dead in my tracks. "Are you serious? What does he mean, prepare the way? Like, for a king?"

"I don't know. That's what I heard. Odd character. His clothes are camel's hair and he lives in the wilderness, they say, like a hermit."

"Is he an Essene?" I asked. "No one seems to know. But he makes his way to the Jordan every day."

"Do you think?" I paused. *Could it be? Dare I say?*

"What?"

"Do you think it's the prophet?" As the whispered words released, I felt my heart pound in my ears.

Just before sundown we gathered for the first Shabbat meal. I shared the rumor with my family. My father stopped sharpening the knife he'd been working on and stared at me.

Slow and quiet, he spoke one word, "Elijah."

My heart raced again.

By the time services ended the next day, the entire village buzzed. The men gathered, as usual, and we all talked at once. Voices pitched in excitement as speculation rose. The older men paused often and looked heavenward. Jesus was with us, of course. I noted he didn't join the conversation.

"What do you think, Jesus?" I asked.

"What do _you_ think, Justus?"

"Well, I think it _could_ be true." _Do I?_ Suddenly I needed courage. I looked at my friend. "Right, Judah? Don't you think it's Elijah?"

"Absolutely."

And then everyone shouted affirmations. The conversation heightened to a frenzy.

I never did hear Jesus' answer.

That evening some of us made a plan to visit the Jordan ourselves. That decision was the beginning of radical change in me.

Since we had some time yet before Fall planting, we agreed to take ten days – four days out, two in the Jordan River region, and four back. My father and brothers, some nephews, and neighbors made up our party. Jesus went, too.

News travels fast around here. Along the way, we met scores of people who also wanted to see the display at the Jordan. Speculation was rampant. Hope was high. Our steps were quick. I made a mental note that Jesus remained peculiarly pensive.

The scene from the summit of the mountain that overlooked the river made me dizzy. Hundreds of people stood in rows five deep at the shore. About ten of them were in the water, in a circle around one man at their center. It was his voice, not the hundreds gathered, that reached us. As we descended, that voice became more clear.

He quoted scripture. It was the Prophet Isaiah. "Get everything ready for the coming of the Lord. Everyone will see God's salvation." And then he said, "I am the voice that cries out in the wilderness." He called for people to repent. But not the kind of repentance that we knew about - the kind that had to be done over and over again. No, he preached that the Redeemer would soon come and that we needed to prepare our hearts for his arrival. The rocky path couldn't slow us. We nearly tumbled down the mountainside. That strange quickening zipped through my heart again. *Is it true?*

Soon we were close to the man dressed in camel's hair, with unruly hair, just as described. We listened, mesmerized. The passion in his unnaturally loud voice confirmed that he believed every word he spoke. Our ears filled with the message they longed to hear.

"Get everything ready for the coming of the Lord!" He preached for us to stop cheating our neighbors and stop wanting things that didn't belong to us. In a nutshell, he told us to live the Mosaic Law of morals and righteousness.

The hot sun tiptoed toward the western sky; its brightness peeked through clouds that kept us cool. His voice penetrated my being. His words pierced my heart. My eyes brimmed, filled with sadness at how I lived my life. *What example have I given my children?* The thought broke my heart. I wove through the throng of fellow pilgrims; we all longed for freedom. Refreshing coolness lapped over my feet as I waded closer to the prophet in the river.

"Here I am! I am a sinner. Cleanse me!" I called to the man with a hyssop branch. He turned to me and waved me further into the moving water. When I reached him, the water was at my waist.

"Do you repent of your wicked ways?"

"Yes, I do!"

"Do you long for the coming of The Messiah?"

"With all my heart," I whispered.

"Then be cleansed. Go on your way and sin no more." And with that, he plunged the hyssop into the water and then shook it violently over me. I lifted my arms and raised my face to the heavens.

How do I feel? Clean? Yes, but so much more. Free? Yes, I'm free! My lips stretched into a smile that nearly split them.

As I came up out of the river, my father and brothers hurried toward the man named John. As in a dream, I watched my family and friends' faces light up as they, too, experienced a spark of true freedom.

When they came up out of the water, we embraced as though we hadn't seen each other in years. *We are new.*

Though we wanted to shout and jump for joy, John continued to preach, even as the sun dipped. We focused on him. He stopped abruptly in mid-sentence, and shifted his gaze. His voice changed to one of awe and surprise as he called out, "Look, here is the Lamb of God! He will remove the sin of the entire world."

As one body, my father, siblings and I turned to see Jesus walk through the water to John. My eyes widened. My mouth dropped open. *What does he mean? What is Jesus doing?*

John continued, "I mentioned him earlier. I told you that after me there would come a man who is greater than me because he existed before me. I didn't know who he was, but the reason I started to baptize in water was so that he could be revealed to Israel."

Jesus? Jesus is the Lamb of God? The One we've waited for? My mind muddled with a thousand questions.

And then Jesus asked John to baptize him.

John stood spellbound for a few moments. He found his voice again, "Why are you doing this? I should be baptized by you."

And Jesus answered, "It's okay. Many things, all righteousness, must be fulfilled. This is the right thing to do for now."

John bowed his head briefly before he thrust the hyssop branch into the river and shook it over Jesus.

I had many sins to be cleansed of. Have I ever seen Jesus say or do anything that could warrant a need for repentance? Surely not.

Yet Jesus looked as refreshed as everyone else baptized by John. And just as he came up out of the water, wearing a hint of a smile, the remnants of the sun broke majestically through the clouds, and a dove that seemed to come from the sun itself flew onto Jesus' shoulder. Before I could question the sight - and I'm not exaggerating when I say this - a voice that thundered from the skies themselves spoke, "This is my son, whom I love. I am fully pleased with him."

Jesus raised his eyes toward the heavens, as did John. My eyes followed their gaze to a glorious peach lining of every dazzling white cloud.

When I spun back to look at Jesus, the dove was gone. I reached my hand out to him, "Jesus?" I didn't recognize my own meek voice.

His eyes danced as he nodded acknowledgment to me, but he continued past me and disappeared into the crowd.

I couldn't wait to share the excitement with my friends. But my amazement did not reflect in their eyes. *What? Didn't they see the dove and hear that voice? The voice that claimed him as son the way a father claims his own?* Dismayed and confused, I kept quiet.

After Jesus' baptism, the sun continued its rapid race to the finish line of the horizon, painting us in soft pinkish orange. Our immediate party headed to my cousin's house, where we stayed. Jesus did not return with us. I won't go into detail about how excited we all were and how much we shared that night. Suffice it to say, we fell asleep not long before the first cock crowed.

When the second cock crowed, we hurried back to the banks of the Jordan for at least a little more of John's enlightened preaching. When we had no choice, we pulled ourselves away from the region for home. We couldn't find Jesus. I wanted to tell him how different I felt. And I wanted to tell him that I saw the dove and heard the voice. *The voice of his father?*

That day in the Jordan transformed my life forever. I decided right then that, even though it seemed we couldn't survive without cheating, I would trust the guidelines of Mosaic Law. And guess what? Living as a man of integrity didn't make life any harder on my family than before. But things were different. Peace inside of me ruled over the worries: no more internal wrestling matches between the reality of being a cheat while I proclaimed to be a good Jew. And, I began to see myself as a good provider who did my best.

When Jesus returned to Nazareth, it was on a Sabbath. I recognized added confidence as he strode into the synagogue. He picked up the scroll and read, "The Spirit of the Lord is within me. For the sake of all, God anointed me to announce good news to those who are poor. He sent me to proclaim that those who are imprisoned will be released. Those who are blind will see. Those who are broken will be forgiven. I publicly proclaim that this is the time ordained by the Lord." The place was more silent than ever as he closed the book and ended with, "What you have heard today brings this scripture to its complete fulfillment."

When his discourse ended, many faces around me reddened with anger, which matched raised voices. For me, I knew at that moment who he was. My head spun with pictures of us growing up together, so I didn't hear why he stirred up such wrath. In fact, I didn't get to talk to him afterward. He enraged so many people that he left town, almost secretly, before dawn.

At last, the words of our ancient leader Joshua made total sense. Others can choose to follow their desire for money or land or power. But as for me and my household, we choose to follow the Lord. It is the best decision our family ever reached together. No longer are we driven by greed or lack of forgiveness. No longer do we seek revenge on those who make life difficult. Worry and fear are no longer companions. Instead, joy and peace from within sustain us through the good days and the bad. Thanks be to God!

Based on the stories in Matthew 3:13, Mark 1:1-11, Luke 3:1 - 4:19, and John 1:19-34

6 ♦ His Secret
Changed My Life

Household staff hear gossip of the entire region almost before news reaches heads of those households. Rumors of some man named Jesus who traveled throughout Galilee teaching on the Holy Scriptures were rampant. Many people considered themselves his followers, even those who used to follow John the Baptizer. The shift in loyalty miffed some of John's disciples. I heard that John actually encouraged the shift and called himself a follower of Jesus. I hoped for a chance to discover the attraction.

Before Ephraim's birth, his wealthy father employed me. Ephraim grew up to be a righteous man, which made my transition to him as master easy. Soon after our move to the dwelling attached to his father's house, he planned to begin his own family.

Ephraim's small staff worked for weeks to prepare for his wedding feast. We gathered pomegranates and almonds, pressed olives, stuffed grape leaves, made sure there was enough wine on hand, brought in the lamb, and much more.

Because my master and his betrothed came from large families, we delivered many invitations to the joyous event. As the people arrived, my concern mounted that we might not have enough food and drink since, unlike his father, Ephraim was of humble means.

From the bride's home of Nazareth came a widow named Mary, a distant relative. I was assigned to serve her son Jesus and his friends. *What good fortune!* I sought him out right away. "Teacher? More wine?" He looked directly into my eyes, as though I were an equal and the only person present. I couldn't force my eyes to glance away. He spoke to me as a friend, which made me feel warm inside. Somehow, the heavy workload of the celebration became light.

On the morning of the eighth day the bridegroom introduced his unveiled bride to the guests. The consumption of food and wine increased as the happiness of the guests heightened.

The next day, my worst fears came true. A worried murmur hummed among the servants. "No more wine."

"Were we irresponsible?"

"Did we waste the provision?"

We were afraid to tell the steward. We knew we'd be punished, whether or not we were the cause.

Within moments our plight reached the women's celebration. *How do the women always know what's going on whether or not they're directly involved?*

A few minutes later, the mother of Jesus approached me. "Is it true? There is no more wine?"

With my eyes cast down, I trembled and hoarsely whispered, "Yes."

Without another word, Mary made an about face and headed to the men's section.

Back at the entrance, I gasped at the scene before me. The bridegroom looked up just as she reached Jesus. But my master said nothing.

I entered the celebration and acted busy by gathering empty platters. *Whatever does she intend? I have to hear what she says to him.*

"There's a problem with the wine. They've run out."

"Woman, why trouble me with this?" Jesus questioned her curiously. "It's not my time yet."

My mind whirled as I scurried to my station. *What did that mean?* I reached my friends and turned to see Jesus behind Mary. They walked directly toward us. I had an urge to run. Or bow. Fortunately, I kept my head and stood tall.

She didn't smile as she measured her words to us, "Just do whatever he tells you to do."

He pointed to six stone jars that stood nearby. "Fill them with water," he gently commanded.

The jars were used for the rites of purification, and could each hold twenty to thirty gallons. We scampered out with them and filled them to the brim. Stunned with wonder, we didn't breathe a word as we returned and set them before Jesus.

"Now," he said with a smile, "draw some, and take it to the steward." He chose the servant with the longest family affiliation for the task: me.

Careful not to allow my shaking hands to spill the water, I served the steward. *Now I really wish I could close my eyes and run.* My head felt like someone slapped me dizzy, and my breath caught when he looked at me, alarmed. He signaled for the bridegroom to join him. *I have surely lost my job.*

"Everyone serves the best wine first," the steward told Ephraim. "Later, after the guests have had plenty to drink, they serve the cheaper wine. But you have saved the best wine until now."

What did I just hear?

The bridegroom raised the cup slowly to his lips. He sipped. He smiled as he lowered the cup and glanced quizzically toward Jesus, who had re-joined his friends. *He must remember that Mary called Jesus from the party.*

"Serve this good wine, then." It was his only response before returning to his celebration.

From that day, I learned all the news I could about the teacher named Jesus of Nazareth. He knew something that I intended to discover. Thankfully, my master shared my quest. It was only a few years before we were honored to learn his secret that changed us completely, like water into wine.

Based on the story in John 2:1-11

7 ♦ Before I Knew Him, He Loved Me

Do I hear a mammoth swarm of honey bees? I staggered from my cave into the blinding light as fast as my broken body could carry me. I squinted to discover what made that sound.

People - hundreds of them. They chattered as they followed a man who strode down the mountain paths.

Before I wondered a minute longer, I stumbled toward him. *Am I crazy? I'm not allowed near anyone. No!* I begged myself. *Don't go. It's certain death.* But my feet ignored my plea.

It seemed an eternally long walk. I hobbled along and called out, "Unclean! Unclean!" People scattered. Panting, I ended up in front of the stranger, a teacher. To compensate for my bowed back, with all the effort I could muster, I turned my head to the side to look up to his face.

He didn't run. He didn't curse me for my approach. In fact, he didn't say a word.

I didn't plan one thing that day. I knelt before him.

"Lord, if you are willing, you have the power to make me clean." *Who said that? Me?* I asked a stranger for the impossible. Yet, something inside of me believed it was my chance to be healed.

When he stretched his hand to touch my face my heart skipped a beat and my head began to swirl. *It's been too many long years since I've felt a person's touch.*

Like healing oil to fresh wounds, his words flowed into my heart. "I will."

I will? He said, I will? I only had to ask and he said, yes?
"Be clean."

And with that simple command, a tingling sensation coursed through my body. Giddy and light-headed, I tried to make sense of what was happening.

The crowd that had steered clear of me gasped when I rose from my knees and stood perfectly straight, face to face with him.

There's no pain in my back. I looked at my hands. I pushed up my baggy sleeves. *My skin is clear and clean.* I raised my arms high. *And I can extend my arms above my head. My feet are pain-free, too. They want to dance! A stranger just healed me and delivered me from exile of family and friends.*

Indescribable happiness and thanks flooded me. My throat tightened. After many minutes of wonder, words escaped, "Lord, thank you. Thank you!"

He smiled.

"Who are you?"

"I am The Light. I am Jesus. Now go and show yourself to the priest. Make the offering Moses commanded. It's important for the people to see the Truth."

"Yes, Lord! Yes! Anything you say, Lord!"

It's been many years since the day Jesus healed me and changed my life forever. Before I knew him, he healed me. Before I knew him, he cared enough to stop and listen to my plea. I only needed to ask.

Based on the story in Matthew 8:1-4

8 ✦ No Longer Thirsty

ow did my life come to this point? Each day I asked myself the same question as I trudged out of the city, alone as usual. *I'm lonely and I'm lost. What have I been searching for my whole life? I've made so many bad choices. I have no friends.* People close their doors when they hear my anklets jingling down the street. They whisper to one another when they see me, and spit out my name, Photina, like a curse. They pull their children close, to protect them from brushing against my garments. I am an outcast.

On one particular morning the air was crisp. It made me hopeful. *Hopeful for what? I constantly long for something. A new life? Why do I bother with such thoughts? The turquoise sky is as stainless as the water I will fill my bucket with. The sky would be pretty if I didn't see it through the veil of a scarred and stained life.* At the sixth hour I headed to the bottom of the mountainside on the edge of Sychar. *The air is warm from the dazzling sun; it comforts me like a blanket around my tired shoulders.*

God promised our forefather Abraham that his descendants would be more numerous than the particles of all the dust in the land and they would be blessed. I swept my eyes across the arid landscape as dust swirled around my wool hem. *Though we hold that promise in our hearts, it's hard to imagine such a number. It's even harder to believe for the blessing. Many long years after the promise to Abraham, God visited our forefather Jacob in a dream. Several times each day I visit Jacob's ancient well by the field he gave to his son Joseph. Yet I have never felt the slightest presence of God anywhere in this dry land. Oh, what I would sacrifice for even the smallest sense of purpose and peace that Jacob knew after his encounter.*

As I approached the well those endless longings rolled through my mind. *There's a man at the side of the stone well.* His elbows propped on his knees. His head rested in his hands. *A weary traveler. Naturally, I'll offer him a drink of this cold and refreshing spring water.*

When I got closer, I could see he didn't wear the garments of Samaritan men. *This man is a Jew!* Since the days of the prophet Ezra when he built the temple in Jerusalem, we Samaritans have not associated with Jews. We even built our own temple to worship on this mountain, though today it's in ruins. I can barely follow the thread of history that caused the separation. What I do know is that Jews only trade with us in an emergency, and we wouldn't even offer the favor of a cool drink to a thirsty sojourner.

I ignored the stranger as I stepped up to the well, yanked the rope over, hooked it to my bucket, and slowly lowered it. I closed my eyes for a moment and breathed in the cool air at the top of the well. It's freshness made me smile inside. I felt the tug of the bucket's weight, opened my eyes, and began to drag it up. And that is when this Jew spoke to me. The shock wasn't just a man speaking to an unknown woman. It was a Jew speaking to a Samaritan.

"Give me a drink."

Startled, I replied, "I'm a Samaritan woman. You Jews have condemned us and everything we have. Don't you know it's against your law to ask me for a drink?"

"Obviously, you don't understand the gift of God. And, you have no idea who just asked you for a drink. If you did, you would have asked him, and he would have given you water that never stops flowing, as though it lives."

What's wrong with this man to talk like that? The noon sun on his tired body has relieved him of his senses. "Sir, you don't have anything to draw water with to give me a drink. Can't you see how deep the well is? Just where are you going to get this water that never stops flowing?" I muffled a laugh. "Our patriarch, Jacob, dug this well. His sons drank from this well. So did his sheep, and goats, and cattle. You don't think you're better than Jacob, do you?"

"Anyone who drinks of the water from this well will get thirsty again. But if someone drinks the water I give him, they will never get thirsty again. The water I give will become a spring of water that bubbles up and overflows into eternal life."

"Sir, give me this water," I replied with wonder. "That way I won't get thirsty anymore and have to walk all this way so many times a day. It's hard work pulling a jug of water up the well."

I don't really understand what he's saying. When I need water, I come to this well. Over and over again. If I could never thirst again, certainly my days would be easier. But there must be more to what he said. What is a spring of water that bubbles up and overflows to eternal life? Stop! I yelled at myself inwardly. Stop yourself from these crazy thoughts. Just take the water he offered.

"Go home. Get your husband and come back." His words slammed at my thoughts.

My heart sank. My head dropped. *This is where I lose my chance at water that keeps me from being thirsty. The end of my chance for an easier life. I have no choice but to tell the truth; whatever I say can be verified or not by any one in Sychar.* After what seemed an eternity, I kept my eyes lowered and whispered, "I don't have a husband."

"That's right. You've had five husbands. And you didn't marry the man you're living with now."

Why didn't he also condemn me like every other person I've met? Besides, how can this Jew possibly know about my life anyway? What else does he know?

"Sir, I can tell that you are a prophet. Our ancestors built a temple to worship on this mountain. But you Jews say that the temple in Jerusalem is the correct place to worship." And then he really astounded me.

"Believe me, woman. There will soon come a time when no one will worship the Father either in your temple or the temple in Jerusalem. But it is already the time when true worshipers worship the Father in spirit and in truth. Those are exactly the ones the Father wants to worship him. God is spirit. Anyone who wants to worship him must do so in spirit and in truth. You Samaritans don't understand who you worship. We Jews do understand because the savior of the world will come from the Jews."

"I know the Jews say that The Messiah is coming. They call him the Christ, the Anointed One. They say that when their messiah comes, he will explain everything."

"He is speaking to you right now."

My heart pounded. My mind spun like a rapid-moving whorl at work. *Who is he? I know the Christ will come from the Jews. This man is a Jew. What does he mean when he said, he's speaking to me right now? Could he be the Christ?* Just as I found my voice to ask, a group of Jews approached.

They came from Sychar and carried sacks. With quizzical expressions, they walked over to the man at the well. I'm sure they wondered why their friend was talking to a Samaritan woman. Rather than speak, one of the men opened a sack and handed him some bread.

The stranger at the well kept his eyes fastened on me for a moment. I stared back at the man who had not shunned me for my wicked life and who even stirred a spark of hope in my soul. *I know those eyes.*

At that instant I left my water jar at the well, whirled around and flew to the city. My feet carried me like wings of a dove, my cloak flapped behind me. With the courage of Judith, one of my favorite women in ancient Scripture, I sped to face those who had alienated me for years. I must have looked as different as I felt because my neighbors didn't turn backs on me. Rather, they rushed to greet me.

"What happened, Photina? Your face is as bright as the sun." Questions and comments full of amazement rained on me.

Breathless, I answered, "You need to come see this man. He knew everything about me. Do you think he could be the Jews' Messiah?"

It was the first time the thought that he might be The Messiah escaped my lips. As the words spilled out, it was as though fire burned through my soul. And then a rush of wholeness – like everything that was broken in me was instantly mended. I was dizzy with wonder and delight as the words of Judith sprang from my mouth, "I will sing to God a new song: O, Lord you are great and glorious."

My news spread like a flood through the city. Not one waited to ask another but with one impulse, we all sped to the well.

His friends were gathered around him; they leaned in to hear him. We stopped short of them, and waited with our eyes averted. We couldn't help but hear him and looked around at each other, fascinated by what we heard. "My food is to do the will of my Father who sent me. He sent me to complete his work. Do you not say, 'There are yet four months, then comes the harvest?' I tell you, lift up your eyes, and see how the fields are already white for harvest."

At that point his arm swept toward Sychar.

Though he saw us, he didn't stop the lesson. "Even now, those who gather the harvest are receiving their wages. In fact, they are receiving fruit that will sustain them into eternal life. There is an old saying, 'One person sows the seed, but someone else gathers the harvest.' It is true even now. Because others, like Moses and the Prophets, preceded you, sowing seeds of the knowledge of God. Now, it is harvest time, and I am sending you to gather in the harvest of those who sowed. In this way, you work together."

He stopped and looked straight into my face. Again, peace caressed my heart. And though his words puzzled me, somehow I knew that in time all Truth would be revealed. He addressed me, "You have brought your neighbors."

"Yes, Lord. I told them what you said to me and they believe like me." It occurred to me that I still didn't know the name of this Jew who knew everything I ever did.

My neighbors received his smile as a welcome. They inched their way toward him as his disciples stepped back to make space. They asked questions that tumbled one on top of another. He answered each with tireless patience. They begged him to come to our city and stay in order to share with those who had not heard. He and his disciples stayed two days with us. For two days Jews stayed in the homes of Samaritans, ate their food and drank their wine - a miracle. Many believed because of his words.

The people of Sychar said to me, "When you told us that you thought you had met The Messiah, we were doubtful. Now that we have heard him teach, we know you were right. This man is truly the Savior of the world."

The Savior of the world, a Jew, asked a favor of me at the well left by Jacob our father. And when I learned his name, the decades-old memory of the frightened young family who fled Bethlehem to protect their son rose to my mind's eye. *Yes, I had looked into those eyes before!*

Those eyes belonged to Jesus of Nazareth – the Christ. He accepted me just as I am, a sinner and a Samaritan. He set me free and made me new. Forever I will give thanks to Him who gave me life. He is my joy and my hope.

Based on the story in John 4:4-42

9 ✦ No Better Friend

Peter welcomed me into his home after the death of my husband because he wanted to, not because he had to. I love my son-in-law. His generosity knows no bounds. Still, if he were not a successful fisherman, I'm not sure he could manage the needs of so many in our household.

About a year ago, our welfare was at risk. Or so I thought, the day he greeted us with a new light in his eyes. His announcement shocked me.

"I have met a rabbi who teaches profound ideas. He chose me as one of his disciples and I said, yes!" And, out of character for Peter, he took my hand and locked his eyes with mine. In his typical straightforward manner, he put my heart at ease, "I know this is a good decision. Don't be afraid. We shall not want."

Peter put capable men in charge of his boats, and made arrangements for a small share of profits. He moved our household from Bethsaida to Capernaum, closer to one of the most profitable fishing sites in the region. He was right. Even after he started work with the teacher named Jesus of Nazareth, all of our needs were met.

Peter and the others who followed Jesus traveled all over Galilee and Judea. They stayed at our house when they were in Capernaum. It was like home to them. My daughter, Abigail, was grateful I shared the increased workload caused by their regular visits. I never minded the effort because Jesus was the kindest and most respectful person I have ever met. His friends treated us with dignity, too.

One week in particular I got it into my head that the house needed extra cleaning. For some reason, even though we had no word that the men would be by anytime soon, I scrubbed and re-scrubbed the ceilings and walls. I wiped down every bench at our long table more than once. Our humble home twinkled spotless. Every day I pressed olives, and made enough oil for several small jugs plus many jars of hummus.

"Mother, stop," my daughter pleaded. "Whatever has gotten into you to clean and work like this? Do you know something I don't?"

"No, no," I smiled into her sweet face. "I am just full of joy that makes it easy for me to work. I want to be prepared for anything."

Perhaps my frenzied efforts were too much for my old body. Toward the end of the week, I needed frequent mid-day rests. One morning I couldn't rise from my pallet, with no power even to roll over. It was all I could do to open my eyes. I shivered though the air was hot. My daughter placed cool, wet cloths on my forehead. The day dragged on.

The next day, screaming from dreams that frightened me interrupted my fitful sleep. My eyes ached to open. I didn't recognize Abigail. She tried to feed me broth and herbal teas. They made me nauseous. She wiped my forehead and wrists over and over. Pain pounded every joint in my body.

I squinted in the darkened room as another cloth attempted to lower my fever. *Is that Jesus in front of me?* My heavy eyes shut and I drifted back into a sea of both cold and hot rushing waves that undulated through me. A sudden tingling, that started in my hand, coursed through me like a fast-moving stream. Peace enveloped me like a warm blanket. My eyelids opened to the kind face of Jesus. His dark eyes penetrated mine. I was refreshed, like I had sipped a cup of cool water on a stifling summer day. I smiled. "Jesus, you healed me."

He didn't say a word. He just returned my smile, took my hand, and helped me stand. My legs were not wobbly, my mind no longer confused, and not one muscle or joint ached.

My family laughed with relief and joy. I wanted to dance with thanks as I served him and his disciples that evening.

As usual, many people found their way to Jesus all through the night. They were healed of illnesses and set free of demons. I can only imagine that their lives were as changed as mine.

Now I meet each day with the certainty that with Jesus as our friend, I have nothing to fear.

Based on the story found in Matthew 8:14-17

10 ♦ Thankful For
Friends Who Believed First

My brothers and I followed the footsteps of our father, a successful fisherman. We provided well for our families. Our homes, larger than any farmer's or artisan's houses, were comfortable. Food abounded.

All that changed about a year ago when I contracted a fever that swept through town. It was a frightening few months, filled with great sorrow. Many children died. Some adults were left with disabilities. Like me.

Overnight, I changed from strong and husky to thin and paralyzed from the waist down. Instantly, our household changed from lively and carefree to a place where worry and lack smothered our thoughts and moods. Our son, whose young family lived with us, took on the financial burden of everyone. My wife, always a fine helpmate, along with two of our daughters, began selling needlework to those who lived like we used to. Our young sons, employed by my brothers, worked longer hours and did harder work than most their age.

What did I do? With glazed eyes, I stared, day in and day out, at the struggle of life around me, and yearned for a day when I'd be the active head of my household again. Unending pain like knife wounds in my unmoving legs was nothing compared to that of my broken heart and spirit. No longer did my robust laughter fill the space around me. Fitful attempts to sleep replaced long and productive nights on the water. Nights dragged into longer, joyless days. With each passing season, I sank lower into a great pit of darkness.

My immediate family and my brothers never gave up on me. They cheered me and found ways to include me in aspects of work. Occasionally all four of my brothers carried me on a pallet to the shore, propped my back against a boulder, and brought nets to me for mending. Clean, salt air freshened my mind as I listened to the waves crash and gazed at the distant horizon. Those hours were life-giving. They made me long to sail again. I can never express my intense gratitude for my brothers' efforts. I was an enormous interruption in their day.

Before the attack on my physical body, a prophet named John had been preaching at the Jordan River about the coming of our Redeemer. He told the crowds they needed to repent and prepare their hearts for his arrival. My brothers, my oldest son, and I trekked to the Jordan. He called for people to step into the river and let him cleanse our sins with living water; we responded without hesitation. The experience gave me hope that soon our people would no longer live under the iron hand of the Romans and that we would be set free of hundreds of years of tyranny. I stopped fretting with anger over the constant tax increases. A thought burned into my heart: *soon, everything will change for good.*

Within weeks of my baptism, the fever swept through Capernaum. My little light of hope extinguished.

Later, rumors reached me about a man named Jesus who showed up at the Jordan one day. John, the Baptizer, announced that Jesus was the Lamb of God. Jesus went to John for baptism like everyone else. They said John didn't want to perform the baptism because he said Jesus should have been baptizing him instead. Then Jesus said something about fulfilling righteousness. No one knew what it meant but everyone present remembered it well.

Stories flew after that. Jesus traveled all over Galilee and Judea like no other rabbi. He did crazy things like turning water into wine at the wedding of a friend. And he healed people. No kidding. Blind men could see; deaf men could hear. I had plenty of time each day to ponder every new story. And to pray about what it all meant.

My thoughts ran the gamut from total disbelief to real possibility. At every Shabbat – the meal to bring in the Sabbath - I brought up my evolving thoughts. It became apparent to me that he was more than just another prophet. He was, as the Baptizer said, the Lamb of God – our Redeemer. Soon every member of my family believed with me.

I kept secret my determination to meet him, somehow. I needed a miracle.

It seemed like all of Galilee came to Capernaum the day that changed my life again. Jesus was home and everyone, especially the Pharisees, wanted a piece of him. Word had it that they were skeptical at the least. At the most, they were ready to accuse Jesus of ultimate crimes against God.

One morning I approached my brothers when they returned from their catch. "Judah. Simon. Nathan," I looked directly at each of them. They each responded with the same quizzical look.

"Jesus is home."

"Yes. And, so?"

"And I want to see him. It's time."

They smiled as they caught each other's glance. Simon spoke first, "Benjamin, we have been wondering how long before you would ask."

"Really?" *They've been waiting for me?*

They nodded in agreement. Nathan, the oldest among us, stepped toward my pallet and shook my hand. "Yes, Benjamin. We know who Jesus is and we believe he can heal you."

Strangely, his certainty rattled me. *Can I really be healed?* But I replied, "Then let's find a way."

My brothers were burly and strong, and they had, as I mentioned, carried me to the water's edge and even to our neighborhood synagogue. But Peter's house, where Jesus lived, was at the southernmost end of Capernaum. We lived due north.

"Brothers," doubt began to creep into my heart, "how? You can't possibly carry me all the way. And he will surely not come to our house."

They laughed in unison. "We have waited long for this day. Don't worry about us. We will have the strength to carry you wherever is necessary," Judah boomed.

They all went off to sleep. *This is what family does for family. I am so grateful.*

Later, we all gathered in my courtyard.

"Are you ready?" Nathan smiled with his inquiry.

"I think so." *Am I?*

In order to reach the other side of town, we had to add more distance to the trip by wending through our district to the main thoroughfare. Not one of my brothers complained as I watched their muscles flex and sweat pour from their brows. About half way there, they set me down to rest and drink from the wineskin my wife had sent with us.

"Shall we turn back?" I asked cautiously. "This is much too hard. And perhaps, all for no reason."

They answered as one man with a resounding, "Absolutely not!"

Judah continued, "It's time for your own story of Jesus's healing power."

I closed my eyes and let the pronouncement sink into my heart. *It's my turn.* An image of me fishing once again was clear in my mind's eye.

After all the heavy labor, when we finally turned east again, we saw a large group of people up ahead. *Oh, no.* As we approached, it became obvious we would never even get near the insular – that cluster of houses by Peter's courtyard. We stopped at the edge of the noisy crowd. They set me down and discussed options in a huddle. Nathan made the final decision.

"We have prayed for a miracle for our brother. We found a way. Will we allow anything or anyone to come between Benjamin and his wholeness? No! But the reality is that, even if we get all the way to the front of the crowd, we still won't be able to reach Jesus. No worries. I've been here before and I know there are steps to the roof. We'll take him up the steps, remove a few tiles of thatch and lower him in."

I know my eyes bulged in astonishment that they would go to this much trouble. *They truly believe!*

They guided me through the crowd, and followed Nathan's plan. It was our last hope.

I gripped the sides of the pallet as they lowered me into the house. My heart beat out of my tunic. I hyperventilated. A few men noticed us and rushed forward to help me land gently. My brothers jumped down into the room and stood by me with their arms folded. We were at the feet of Jesus. I closed my eyes. The room fell silent. *I hope we made the right decision.*

I opened my eyes, then, and looked directly at a face as peaceful as the sea in mid-summer with eyes soft as those of a young doe. "Jesus," I whispered.

His eyes glided from me to each of my brothers. Their faces were solemn but their eyes twinkled with expectancy as he smiled and nodded at them. The doe eyes returned to my face. I could only think, *I'm ready for whatever gift you would give me, Jesus.* His next words caught me off guard.

"All is forgiven. Any sins you have ever committed are all forgiven."

My sins? But before I had a split second to consider the words, through my body swept a rush like a great wind. I shuddered as it changed to an intensely hot, tingling up and down my legs.

I was only slightly aware of the scribes and Pharisees arguing that only God could forgive sins. Sensations that raced through my body distracted me. *Am I awake or asleep?*

And then, like a distant ship's bell sounding far off in the night, I heard, "Man." *He's calling me.*

I squinted into his face, as though forcing myself to awake from a deep sleep, "Yes, lord?"

"Stand up. Pick up your bed and go home."

The crazy tingling increased as it spread from my legs throughout all of me. Without taking my eyes off Jesus, I leaped to my feet. My head began to spin. I waited just a moment before bending to pick up my pallet. I got up and faced him again. He smiled at me and nodded to my brothers.

Tears sprang from my own eyes when I looked into theirs that glistened. *They never doubted what Jesus could do for me.* And then they moved toward me for a huge group hug. The room filled with laughter, praise, and, sadly, some angry voices. My own voice was loudest, "Glory to God in the highest!"

My brothers led me to the door and I glanced over my shoulder at Jesus whose gentle eyes stayed on me. Respectfully, I lowered my eyes and dipped my head briefly in thanks.

I am a successful fisherman again and provide well for my family. But I am a changed man. No longer do I only think of God when I want something or when I hear Scripture recited. Inside is a joy that causes me to praise and thank Him every single day for his mercy.

Based on the story in Luke 5:17-26

11 ♦ Real And Lasting Change

My parents gave birth to an embarrassment - me. I'm so grateful they loved me anyway. They could have turned me out with no blame. After all, who can afford the burden of a deformed child?

From age three, when I was weaned, I recall the looks and stares wherever I went. The most blunt remarks were from the youngest and most innocent neighbors.

"Mother, look. Why can't he hold the cup like me?"

"Why does his hand look so funny?"

"What's wrong with him?"

"He scares me." Their faces scrunched up and their eyes grew wide just before they ran away.

At six I was excluded when the neighborhood boys went to our little school. "Why teach a disfigured boy to read? He'll only be a beggar someday," I heard more than once.

For years, I deceived myself into thinking that when I hung my head no one could see me. But as the boys around me got older, they made sure I knew the reality. "Where'd you get your hand stuck?" Or, "Don't come near me. I don't want to catch whatever it is you have." Each day I held back my tears until bedtime where I wrapped myself tightly in my cloak and stifled sobs into my arm.

When everyone else helped with chores, I was left out. I couldn't do what most sons did for their families. I learned to hate myself.

More than going to school or running with the other boys, I wanted to be just like my father. Each day he left at dawn; I smiled and waved, then turned my head before he saw my glassy eyes. By age 12, most boys apprenticed with their fathers or uncles. Father's height and muscular arms gave him an advantage that made him an in-demand day laborer. He worked hard as a mason, proud to provide well for us. He made me proud, too.

The "normal" boys trotted off to work each day with their fathers, jostling and joking together. Me?

"Go to Jerusalem, Son, where many people live and work," my father instructed. "Find a corner on a busy thoroughfare. Better yet, find a place near the Temple Gate Beautiful. Hold the wooden cup in the palm of your good hand as you wrap your other hand around it, so people can see. They'll pity you." *I don't want pity. I want a life.*

My strong father left each day to work hard. I walked out behind him and began my two-hour journey to Jerusalem with my cup, a piece of flat bread wrapped around olives and a small flask of water. The first few weeks, I walked with my head high. *At least I can contribute to our household.* The pink arms of the sun waving across the earth, led the way. As it rose, golden light washed the fertile land. Walking with the sun as it opened the day made my mornings hopeful. For awhile.

It wasn't long before my head hung and my feet scuffed along the road regardless of the sun's cheery greeting. My eyes stopped enjoying its wonder. By daybreak joy was replaced with intense loneliness as I headed to town with tens of workers whose morning chatter always excluded the outcast.

Every work day for seven years, my body shivered in winter, dripped with sweat in peak summer or endured rain-soaked clothes sticking to me. On dry days I choked, as thousands of feet scuffed up dust into my nostrils. It stung my eyes. More than once, crushed between billows of scratchy linen, the fear of suffocation overpowered me. "Help!" "Watch out!" "Ouch!" It didn't matter what I said or how loud I said it. *I am a non-person; I have no voice.*

I did look forward to a little light in my life at the end of each week, when the sun dipped below the horizon and the Sabbath began. Our first Shabbat meal that heralded its arrival could almost be fun because most of my relatives were kind. I almost felt like I belonged. The next day, Sabbath, was even more of a respite. Not that I enjoyed worship. *Why would I want to worship a creator who gave me a withered hand?* It's that the break from my daily misery refreshed me with courage to meet the next week.

One Sabbath day my life changed forever.

Each night of the week leading up to it, when I dragged myself home, I listened to incredulous stories about some man called Jesus who was in town. In the mornings as I trudged to Jerusalem, I walked closer to the men around me, forced myself out of my solitary thoughts, and eavesdropped.

"Did you see what he did last night?"

"Did you hear him teach?"

"Did you know he healed so and so's daughter who's been sick for so long?"

At first, I didn't know what to make of it all. Finally, I decided he used magic. *He came here to fool people. Probably every healing will be reversed once he leaves town.*

On the Sabbath morning at the end of his first week in town, a buzz hummed through the neighborhood. Jesus had infuriated the Pharisees. Every Jew knew not to lift a hand on the Sabbath. We were not to do anything that resembled work or effort of any kind. That man Jesus and his followers went through the grain fields and actually plucked heads of grain to eat. *How brazen!* Opinions flew as we walked to synagogue. *I don't care what he does. I'm just glad someone's around to distract people from me for a change.*

Just as my family entered the synagogue, we heard an unfamiliar voice vying with the Pharisees behind us. Always at the tail end of our group, I looked over my shoulder at the commotion. What a mistake!

One of the Pharisees walked right up to me and pointed to my hand, "Is it legal to heal someone on the Sabbath?"

A strong but soothing voice replied, "If you had a sheep that fell into a pit on the Sabbath day, wouldn't you pull it out?"

Silence like death filled the air. Dread wrenched my heart. I dropped my head and squeezed my eyes shut, like when I was little. *Maybe this time I really will be invisible.*

The man continued, "A man is so much more valuable than a sheep! So, isn't it legal to do a good deed on the Sabbath day?"

Deafening silence.

I squinted my eyes open. He walked briskly toward me. My eyes sprung wide open when his soft brown eyes looked directly into them and he gently commanded, "Reach your hand out to me."

Should I? He wants me to show him my withered hand. Was this a trick?

His steady gaze quieted my inner turmoil.

Without another thought, I obeyed. And, then, I stopped breathing. At the same moment, as from one person, the entire gathering gasped. *Did I actually show him my good hand?* I quickly pulled up the sleeve of my other hand. *What happened to my withered hand? They're both whole! They look the same! Is this man Jesus the magician?*

The news reached my parents within seconds. They pushed through the gawking crowd that pressed around me. Their eyes were like saucers when they saw my hands. They turned to Jesus. And then back to me. As our eyes met, we all burst into tears, not of shame that I knew so well, but of unbelievable joy!

That very day, two years ago, I asked Father if I could apprentice with him.

"Of course, my son!" He roared with laughter and threw his arm across my shoulder.

Soon I will be a master craftsman just like my father. I earn a good wage. I have friends. I smile. I even sing at the end of a long day at work. I can verify that Jesus is not a magician. I live a life filled with happiness because I did what he asked. I travel to see him whenever he is nearby. I tell everyone I meet how he changed my life. I tell them Jesus will do that for anyone who will listen to him and obey.

Lately I wonder: *Is he the long-awaited Messiah?*

Based on the story in Matthew 12:9-13

12 ✦ He Chose Us

I choked on the dust that swirled around me and filled my nostrils. Unending tears stung my eyes. *I can barely see; I may as well be blind anyway.* The din of wailing and flutes deafened me. The heat of the long day past weighed heavily. It was too hard to lift one foot in front of the other. Arms of friends guided me. Words spun through my head without control. *How can I survive? This can't be real. Who will care for me? Who will help me? Why? Why? Why?*

The procession continued toward the caves. I tried not to look at the face of the young man on the bier. *My son! My only son! The last of my family!* I stole a glance and convulsed into more sobs.

A crowd bigger than our procession approached from behind. Their voices rose, interrupting my despair. *Oh, please, have respect for the dead.* I looked back toward them. One man seemed to lead them. He stopped to face those people with him and raised his arm to silence them. *Thank you.*

In a few moments, he reached my side. I sensed him looking at me. In my grief-induced stupor, I slowly turned my head toward him. *Those eyes are full of compassion. He understands my agony.* He slowed his pace to match mine. With a voice that made me think of a cool breeze in the blazing heat of noon he comforted me, "Don't cry."

I stopped. He paused with me. I turned to stare closely into his dark eyes. *Who is this man?* And, then, he reached out to touch the wicker bier. Instantly, everyone halted and stopped wailing. The flutes' melancholy notes strangled and stopped.

"Young man, get up." *Did he really tell my son who is dead to rise as though he is alive?* An involuntary gasp by one and all present confirmed my thought.

My son pushed himself up. The bearers stumbled to lower the bier quickly. *All praise to God!*

"Where am I, mother?" a groggy voice asked as his eyes locked on mine. "What's happening?"

The man who had spoken stepped closer, took my son's hand and held it out for me. I leaped forward and grabbed my son into my arms, "My son! You were dead and now you live!" Tears sprang from my eyes. I glanced behind me at the stranger. He smiled and his eyes twinkled with moisture.

All around me people laughed and cried and danced. The reality of what happened dawned on us, and nearly every man and woman present fell to their knees and called out, "Praise be to God!"

"He has sent a great prophet like Elijah and Elisha before him."

"God has visited us with a great miracle!"

Yes, God has done this. But why did he choose to raise my son and not others? I will never know the answers to those questions. I only know that he did.

Before we re-assembled ourselves, the teacher had moved ahead with a multitude of followers. My neighbors told me his name is Jesus, son of Joseph of Nazareth.

Because I will never forget what he did for my son and me, I live differently. My neighbors notice new compassion in my actions, more than I ever thought I could give. Now I am one in the throngs of people who cluster around him and hang on his words that pierce my heart. And I praise God day and night, for now I know Him.

Based on the story in Luke 7:11-17

13 ✦ Authority Over All Other Authority

I was content with my life. It was my good fortune that, though I wasn't a Roman citizen, I was one of the rare conscripts in the auxiliary. Being a conscript meant that my wages were high and I could do and have whatever I pleased. The older I got, the wiser I grew. One bit of wisdom I acquired had to do with my servants. It proved that if I treated them with even feigned respect, they seemed to enjoy working for me and did a better job. Their devotion led to a peaceful household. Life worked and I enjoyed it. Regardless of the enticing words of the Jewish teacher, I didn't want to change a thing.

Everyone agreed he carried himself with authority like no other Jewish rabbi. Some were afraid of his charisma that attracted a huge following. Others were merely fascinated. Still, the general buzz around our auxiliary unit was that even though we ruled the Jews and were charged to keep an eye on this Jesus character, we might be intrigued by him. Whether that would be good for us or not, no one would venture to guess. Personally, I had a hard time believing in the god of the Jews, but when I listened to that teacher, something inside nudged me. *Should I think about applying some of what he says?*

So, I paid attention as I guarded. He constantly performed miraculous healings. I listened to him speak radically to his own religious leaders. He told his followers it's not their place to judge the actions of others and that only their god is the true judge. And he treated women and children just as he did the men. It looked to me like he believed they actually deserved honor and respect. Many nights, my head spun with wonder as I laid it to rest.

Little by little, as I spent more time near him, changes in my attitudes and actions crept in. I focused first on people's explanations before I jumped to conclusions. Occasionally, I helped the women in my family with simple chores, which, though appreciated, shocked them. I even smiled more often, or so my friends told me.

One day a favored servant came to me with a pale face that dripped of sweat, and red swollen eyes. He held his head with one hand, leaned on the wall with the other, and rasped, "Master, I'm sick with fever. I don't think I can work today."

"Oh, Juba, I'm sorry to hear this. Let me take you to your quarters. I'll call your wife from her work to wait on you." I've known Juba since I was a child. He cared for me, he played with me, he taught me life lessons. When I left my father's house, I asked to have Juba go with me.

For days Dihya cooled Juba with wet cloths and fed him sips of broth. I checked on him each morning. On the third day, we called a doctor. We followed every bit of his advice. But as Juba's fever continued to rage, weight fell off him, and horrific hallucinations played out in screaming and flailing. Fear of the worst filled my household. By the time I heard that Jesus had returned to Capernaum, Juba's body had become paralyzed. *I think Jesus is Juba's only hope.*

Ready to take a step of faith in the person I had come to admire, I sought him out.

Just inside the city gates I came upon a crowd that surrounded the man who had become famous to all. I took a deep breath and made my way to him through the throngs - easy for one who wielded power everywhere. Little did anyone know that this centurion quaked in his boots.

"Lord, my servant lies paralyzed at home. He is tortured with his illness." I hoped only my authority showed, not the trembling inside, as I waited for an answer.

"I will come heal him."

Just like that. No other questions. He heard my plea and took immediate pity. But he caught me off guard. *Wait. He wants to come to my house? Am I worthy to invite him to my house?*

"Lord, I am not worthy for you to enter under my roof. But, only say the word, and my servant will be healed." *I have just publicly stated what I believe privately.* And before more thoughts could form, I continued, "I am a man who understands authority. I have soldiers under me. I say to one, 'Go,' and he goes. I say to another, 'Come,' and he comes. I say to one of my slaves, 'Do something,' and he does it." *And I have just confessed my willingness to come under his authority.*

Jesus narrowed his eyes steadily at me. Instead of responding to me, he astonished everyone by addressing the crowd, "This is the truth: Throughout all of Israel I have not seen such strong faith. I'm telling you, there will be many who will come from the far reaches of the earth to sit and dine in the kingdom of heaven with Abraham, Isaac, and Jacob. But many others who are confident that they should be guaranteed heaven because of their heritage, as descendants of Abraham, will find themselves thrown into outer darkness where sadness and great despair will fill them."

He recognizes my faith. Yes, now I admit that I do have faith in him. I assumed the Jews understood what he said about who goes to heaven and which people will be filled with despair. That part didn't matter to me. What jolted me was that he knew my heart. And then he spun around back to me.

"Go. It will be just as you believed."

I stood motionless. The past few moments were like scattered pieces of a puzzle in my mind; I tried putting them together. Jesus walked away.

"Thank you!" I called after him, hoping he heard me. Then I headed toward home.

Before I reached my villa, Dihya came running toward me, her cloak flying behind her. My heart pounded as I ran to meet her. "Master!" she panted.

"Yes? What is it Dihya? What's happening?"

"It's Juba!"

Though her face was radiant, a thin line of fear sought to strangle my heart.

"He lives! He is well. He is strong. He is healthy again! It's a miracle." She danced a little circle with upraised arms.

I stopped breathing for a split second, as though I had walked into a wall. I looked heavenward. Intense thanksgiving replaced all fear. *It's true. He did what he said he would do.*

The reality is that he healed more than my servant. My whole being changed forever that instant. I found it difficult to execute harsh punishments on people who did no wrong. Without a second thought, I found myself helping people in need, those I ruled over, as well as those in my household. I looked for ways to help my neighbors. And I took to heart every word the rabbi said whenever he was near.

I still did not fully understand who he was until that dreadful day when he was bludgeoned and hung on a cross. That day my heart burst with full knowledge. *Truly this was the Son of God.*

Based on the stories in Matthew 8:5-13 and Luke 7:1-10

14 ✦ White As Snow

I dreamed I'd be a beautiful, well-respected woman of God, valued as rubies like the wife I heard about in Scripture. But my father died when I was just a few months old. His oldest brother took my mother as his wife. On a trade run, robbers killed him. Oh, how the family used to beg him not to travel at night. At eight, the next brother in line took us all in. That's when my dream began to lose its gleam.

Saying three families made a crowded household is a crazy understatement. There was never enough food even though we all worked hard in Uncle's fields. Home life was miserable since everyone bickered noisily. Because we also worked so much in the house, I had little time with my mother.

My uncle was decent but he never treated me as one of his own. For example, he always sided with anyone I disagreed with. He even 'forgot' my treat when he brought them home to the other children. If I was sick, he didn't check on me. No doubt I was nothing more than an obligation. And just when life couldn't be worse, Mother died in childbirth when I was only ten. I cared for my new brother as though he were my own. With face muffled in my arm, I cried myself to sleep every night from the day he was born.

I spent countless unsupervised hours wherever I chose, as long as I finished my work first. I made friends with people I'm certain Mother would not have approved. The people I hung out with were more like family than my blood relatives. We experimented with lifestyles that my heart told me were not good for the soul. Most of us longed for boundaries set by a loving parent. Without that parent, I ventured step by step into a dark world.

At twelve I still wasn't betrothed. I had no idea why. And that was about the time I began to give in to sweet-talking men who cared only for themselves. Though grateful for income I could call my own, I wept as their sin became mine. When my uncle learned how I earned money, he sent me away. To be cast away from my siblings grieved me as much as the loss of my mother. I swam in a sea of self-loathing. Even so, for years I continued to live a disgraceful life.

A teacher from Nazareth began traveling through the region. For many months I listened from a distance when he spoke to a flock of followers. Each time I heard him speak my heart burned with greater remorse than the time before. Eventually, I was overwhelmed by the knowledge of my sin and determined to start fresh. But, how? I tried to change, but my godless ways were all I knew.

One day, I asked around to find out where Jesus was teaching. Late in that pivotal day of my life, I learned that a Pharisee had invited him to dinner. I struggled with a constant urge in my spirit to make a move. Finally I gave in, compelled to risk all.

My precious little alabaster cruse of ointment wasn't expensive, as ointments and unguents go, but it was all I had and I used it drop by tiny drop. Without a plan, I took it from my cupboard, hid it under my cloak, and walked with measured steps to the home of Simon, the Pharisee.

In the courtyard I removed my sandals, and, with head down, walked past his servants whose eyes widened and mouths dropped. My reputation was known far and wide.

At the sight of the men at dinner, tears gushed down my face. My shallow breath didn't match the merciless pounding of my heart. *I feel like I'm dying.*

I approached the feet of Jesus where he reclined on the couch, and knelt behind him. Suddenly, the difference between us became clear. *He is all purity.* I cried harder as I bent over his feet and let my tears wash him. I wiped his feet dry with my long, dark hair, in submission to that purity. Then I broke my precious alabaster and tenderly rubbed the fragrant ointment into his feet. *Thank you,* was all I could think. When I finished bathing his feet, rivulets of release continued down my face. In my heart I begged God for mercy. *Cleanse me. Make me new.* I stayed still, with my head bowed. I breathed normally, but my heart continued to beat furiously. I sat in his presence, aware of only him. How long was I there? I have no idea. What was Simon, the host, doing? I didn't have a clue. And I didn't care.

Dimly, I heard a discussion between Jesus and the Pharisee. Their voices seemed far away. I strained to listen. *It's me they're talking about.*

Jesus said, "Look at this woman." The words swam in and out of my head then scattered like little fish fleeing a net. Finally, I heard, "She has committed many great sins, but they have all been forgiven for she loves greatly. Those who have only been forgiven of a few little sins, only love a little."

Involuntarily, I lifted my head and looked directly into eyes that danced with fire.

"Your past sins are no longer a part of you."

At his words, a wave of unidentifiable force raced over me and through me. *It's like something is washing over me, making me new - like I was dead and now I'm alive!* "Thank you." *Oh, thank you is not enough. But, what more can I say?*

"Your faith has rescued you from destruction. Now, go in peace."

With head bowed, I rose slowly and backed out of the house. A rush of energy coursed freely through my veins, as though they were unblocked for the first time. And then, calm flooded my heart. Like drops of spring rain that cause flowers and trees to burst into bloom, my fresh tears watered new life in my soul. *I am clean and forgiven, white as snow.*

I vowed to myself, right at that moment, to tell everyone I meet about this man who freed me from all disgrace and gave me new

15 ♦ Peace Leads Me

W e roasted all day in the brutal sun as story after story told by my close friend filled our ears. The stories often left me with questions and confusion. But, when he took us aside from the masses to explain the stories, understanding awakened in me like a spark ignites tinder into flames.

At the end of the grueling day, the twelve of us dragged ourselves downhill to shore. It was time to cross the sea once more. Jesus strode ahead and climbed into one of the boats. I joined its crew.

Jesus went directly to the stern and collapsed into sleep. *No wonder he's drained. The day seemed endless.* He taught every minute and answered questions of hundreds of people. It was impossible to keep track of how many.

As the boats shoved off from the beach, we leaned back and reflected on the day's events. As we talked, I considered my feelings. *I wonder why I'm so calm. And confident.* I envisioned myself as a bucket filled to overflowing with the waters of the sea that held all the mysteries of life. *His words are a light into those deep mysteries. If I continue to pay attention, I'll gain more understanding.*

Without warning, as happens often on the Sea of Galilee, gale force winds whipped the waters. Immediately each roll of the waves was higher than the one before, like they wanted to touch the sky. Our boat shook and rocked and threw us off our feet. Rolling black clouds unleashed torrents.

Looking back, I chide myself for not shutting my eyes right then to focus on the contentment that filled my heart all day. What did

I do instead? I closed in on the raging scene before me and allowed it to fill me with fear that strangled my newfound peace. "Jesus! Jesus!" I yelled as I tripped over nets and walked my hands along the side of the boat to the stern. *Water is overtaking us!*

"Teacher, wake up!" I shook his arm.

He squinted open eyes heavy with sleep and stared into mine. *What do I see in his eyes? It's not fear.*

"Don't you care?" I screamed over the howl of the wind, disregarding the fact that he was exhausted. "We're about to die!"

He sighed and pulled himself up, steady despite the tossing boat underfoot.

He glared at the wind and yelled for it to stop. "Peace! Silence!" Then he flashed his eyes at the sea and demanded, "Be still! Quiet!"

In that instant the wind ceased and a great calm swallowed the sea. *What happened? I can hardly believe this.*

And then he faced us with that same unidentifiable look. "Why were you so afraid? Even after all you've seen, you still have no faith?" *It's agony in his eyes and voice.*

His words stung my heart. *For months I've been growing to trust his very presence with us. I'm certain that every word he speaks is Truth. One storm comes along and just like that I allow fear and worry to control me. My heart had finally learned the meaning of love through trust in him. But, now where's my faith? Maybe I have none.* I dropped my head; salty tears burned my eyes.

When I raised my head, I spotted Jesus taking his tired body back to the cushion in the stern. And then we all stared at one another with eyes that held a mixture of bewilderment and awe. "Who is this man? Even the wind and the sea listen and obey him," everyone asked in his own way.

As we steered the boat to the country of the Gerasenes, my confusion lifted. *I know who he is*. Right then, I decided that, regardless of life's storms that will always rise up, my faith in him will guide my thoughts and actions. It's the best decision I've ever made.

Based on the story in Mark 4:35-41

16 ✦ My Only Hope

I knew who he was. Though I would never have admitted it to anyone. And I knew what he could do for me. He was my last hope. For twelve years, I ran to every physician and healer for miles around. Each one assured my healing. Yet I continued to hemorrhage, too weak most days to rise from my pallet. *I have spent every penny I have. I am at the end of all my thoughts. I go through the motions of living but I do not feel alive. I am empty.*

There he goes with his disciples. They're in a hurry. Oh, Jesus, if only I could touch you. As usual, a crowd encompassed them. *No! Get out of my way. Now he's too far away from me. I must get closer again.*

Heedless of the law that in my condition I should touch no one, I lowered my head and hoped no one would recognize me. I wove my way through the sweaty, smelly bodies. I caught my breath as I reached out. *I am certain that even if I just touch the hem of his garment, or one of those blue tassels, I'll be healed.* I closed my eyes and reached past his disciples to do just that.

How can I describe the feeling when all brokenness is instantly mended? It's like everything inside was loose, falling apart and weak and suddenly a healthy, strong body supported me. *Oh, no! He's turning around. Does he know that I, unclean as I am, touched him?*

"Who touched me?"

Help! I need to run and hide. The crowd is too close.

His friends chided him, "How can you ask such a thing? The crowd is pressing against you from all sides."

His gentle eyes panned the crowd. *I have no choice.* Weeping, I fell in front of him with my face to the ground.

"Oh, Lord, forgive me. I have been sick for twelve long years. I have seen every physician for miles. No one could heal me. In my heart I knew that you were my last hope. I knew that if I could just touch your hem I would be healed. Glory to God. It's true. I am totally healed." I held my breath. *Surely, now the rebuke.*

Instead, I felt a hand take mine and raise me up. I looked into dark, serene eyes as this Jesus, my healer, called me "daughter," commended me for my faith, and told me to go in peace and be healed of my disease. In a daze I watched him continue with his friends.

Today I tell my story joyously so that others may also believe. I know God sent this man Jesus. He called me "daughter" and spoke to me as a loving father. I was empty and broken. He filled me with joy and restored me.

Based on the story in Matthew 9:18-22

17 ✦ A Life With Meaning

I gaze into her sparkly, dark round eyes as she snuggles into me. "Oh, little one," I whisper as I rock her slowly. "I hope you will know him as I do. For without him, you would not even be here." Her little eyelids close, her tiny ruby lips part, and her breath is even like the lake's gentle lapping on the shore. I can feel my daughter's security. I have such a story to tell her one day.

When I was little, my father was in charge of our synagogue. He made me so proud. He kept the building and grounds well maintained. Our family was respected and we lived well because of my father's position. Life was as easy for us as possible in an occupied land.

In the years before my betrothal, much unrest grew in Galilee. One day Father took me to buy fish, a trip usually reserved for one of my brothers. I remember every golden moment. I also remember some things that concerned me. He and other customers griped, "It's bad enough that we struggle with taxes that increase almost every day, and that the Romans clamp down on us without warning. Now what? Some itinerant making waves, too? There's a bubbling undercurrent of unrest. Isn't that enough to worry about?"

From what I could tell, there was a teacher called Jesus who traveled from town to town and explained Scripture in most synagogues he came to. That wasn't odd. Teachers often traveled and taught. However, Jesus seemed to know Scripture better than anyone, which irritated synagogue leaders. Gossip was that he angered the Pharisees because they thought he acted like he had more authority than they did. Worse, he actually healed people of all kinds of sicknesses. People were afraid.

I remember the first time he taught in our synagogue. After that, I often noticed my father lost in thought while he walked home from work. And he carried himself differently. He no longer walked that way that made people feel inferior to him. The change in Father was permanent.

One night, after another visit to town by Jesus, Father and Mother talked in hushed tones after the sun hid in the darkness.

"Eunice," Father began, "I can't begin to tell you what it's like to hear him speak. Of all the rabbis I've ever heard, not one speaks with such assurance."

"Really?" she asked.

"Yes. And there's more." His voice lowered, "Caleb and Milcah were there with their youngest child whose eyes were dull and red. They waited at the entrance to the synagogue and when he appeared, they walked directly to him. Milcah carried the girl and Caleb spoke, "Lord, if you would, heal our daughter."

"And then what happened?"

"Without a word, Jesus touched the child's forehead. The second he touched her, she smiled and her eyes shone clear and bright. He looked at Caleb and Milcah and said, 'Your faith has healed your little one. Now, go.'"

"Honestly?" Mother gasped. "Someone in our neighborhood healed?"

"Yes," Father replied solemnly.

I fought the urge to inch my way closer to them.

"What do you think all of this means?" she asked, and leaned in to hear him.

"I'm afraid to wonder."

"What does that mean, Jairus?" she bolted upright in her seat.

"It's as though I'm drawn to him as if he's the ultimate authority."

Mother was quiet. I glanced up from helping my little brother Jonas prepare his mat for bed. Father looked at her in earnest. *She looks worried.*

After that night, I listened closely whenever I was around my father and his friends. I could tell he wanted to convince them to get to know this Jesus because, at the least, what he taught was beyond reproach. They ridiculed him for even hinting that Jesus was greater than other teachers. Always a huge argument ensued. Always, Father let them battle among themselves.

By the time I turned twelve, it had been sometime since my father encountered Jesus and saw our neighbor's miracle. My womanhood approached as did my betrothal to a man agreed to long ago by my parents.

At that time, a fever raged from neighborhood to neighborhood through Capernaum. It wasn't long before the outbreak hit our home. One of my brothers fell ill. Fortunately, like most afflicted, he was back to his rambunctious antics in just a few days.

Then I fell ill. This part of my story my parents told me later.

When the fever attacked me, I didn't heal fast as most others, so my parents called the doctor. They followed his instructions. They tried to fill me with herbal teas, but I couldn't swallow. They cooled me with wet cloths day and night, but I still thrashed and mumbled at things that didn't exist. They said I wasted away before their eyes. Each night when they said goodnight they wept, afraid it would be the last. My fevered delirium lasted through three Sabbaths.

It was about that time they heard that Jesus returned from the eastern shore to stay with his friend, Peter. He often stayed with Peter, whose house was large enough to accommodate Jesus and his friends.

In a desperate move, my father left work at the synagogue early and headed to the shore where Jesus had disembarked. He said he would have gone to Peter's house if needed. And though he looked frantic to those around him, he told me he was perfectly calm inside.

With sweat on his brow, he wove through the typical throng of people that hemmed in Jesus wherever he traveled. At last, he found himself in front of the Teacher. Father told me he didn't think twice before he fell at Jesus' feet to plead, "My little girl is sick and near death. Please come. Lay your hands on her, so that she will recover and live." Jesus looked straight into his eyes with total recognition. He said it seemed Jesus recognized him, almost as he would an old friend. Jesus nodded.

With hope, and thanks that we lived so close to the sea, Father led them through the noisy crowd that squeezed against them.

Suddenly Jesus stopped. "Who touched me?"

Who touched me? Father thought. *There are at least fifty people crushed against us. It could have been anyone. What a crazy question. Let's get going. My daughter is dying!*

Incredibly enough, a woman with head held low approached Jesus. It seems that on purpose she had touched one of his blue tassels. And at the moment she did, the terrible sickness she had been stricken with for twelve years left her body.

Father wondered at the coincidence. *Twelve years. The age of my little girl.*

Jesus said to her, "Your faith has healed you. Go in peace."

They are the same words he spoke to Caleb and Milcah, Father recalled.

Just then, our beloved servant Enos appeared to Father through the swarm of followers. Tears streamed down his face as he gushed the words no parent wants to hear, "Your daughter is dead. Don't bother the Teacher anymore."

"No!" Father felt heat rush into his face as he exploded in agony. His body whirled to face Jesus. His only angry thought, *why did you stop for that woman? You let my daughter die!* But when his eyes met Jesus' eyes, his racing heart slowed and he didn't open his mouth to speak.

"Don't be afraid," Jesus told him, "only believe. She will be saved."

Jesus instructed the mob not to follow. He continued on with Father and three of his friends.

As they travelled, Father repeated to himself over and over, *Only believe. Yes, I believe. That's why I'm here.* His spirits rose. Until they arrived at home.

A great number of people had already gathered inside and out. They wailed loudly or mourned with their flutes. Father's heart sank; he shook and wept.

Still, Jesus remained steady. He walked into the house with that same authority Father recalled at synagogue. He stood in the center of the noisy group and said, "There's no need to cry. The child is not dead. She is merely sleeping." As they laughed at Jesus, he sent them outside.

Father was amazed that a sense of peace overwhelmed him from head to toe. No more fear or anxiety nagged at his heart.

Jesus took Peter, James, John and my parents into the place where I lay still, in a pool of sweat. My shallow breathing was indiscernible. Jesus took my hand.

Now I can continue my story.

When he took my hand, he spoke, "Tal'itha cu'mi - little girl! Wake up!" The clear words penetrated me, from a voice that seemed at once inside of me and outside, too. It was a voice that I knew, though he had never spoken to me before. It coursed through my body and awakened every cell. I blinked and smiled into almond eyes that knew me. And I obeyed. I stood and looked around, wondering why my parents and several strangers stood in the room with me. Their mouths dropped open.

Jesus broke the silence, "Give her something to eat."

My mother rushed forward, gathered me in her arms, and cried in a loud voice, "My daughter lives!" Father moved over and embraced us both. No words came from his glowing face, wet with tears.

They gave me food and drink and even after all those days without eating one morsel, I ate an entire meal. It was as though I had never been sick even one minute. In fact, I was refreshed.

From that day, our entire household believed in the name of Jesus. We knew who he was and every one of us intended to follow him to the ends of the earth. It was a choice that has made all the difference in our relationships, in our work, and in our hearts.

Now I whisper to my firstborn as I rock gently back and forth, "Yes, Tal'itha cu'mi - little one." My eyes rivet on her angelic face. "I pray you will know Jesus, too. For then your life will also have true meaning."

Based on the stories in Mark 5:21-43 and Luke 8:40-56

18 ✦ No Condemnation

ow did I ever become such a disgrace? I loathe myself. My parents' morals were high. We attended synagogue as required. One time I had the sweet opportunity to travel with my family to the temple in Jerusalem. I remember well the long, hot journey because it touched my heart to share the holy pilgrimage with so many. All this to say, because of the moral teachings ingrained in me since birth, I intended to live upright.

At fourteen, I was given in marriage to a man twenty years older than me. His first wife died during the birth of their ninth child. As a silk trader, he provided well for us. Still, the responsibility of nine children and the oversight of a huge household, literally overnight, frazzled me. To make matters worse, his oldest children were my age. Even though this family situation was common, it made me feel awkward.

City life was hard to adjust to, especially over-crowded Jerusalem. In Emmaus, my town, everyone knew and trusted each other. Exhaustion and irritability became my middle names. I still wonder if my overall outlook was the reason my husband spent little time with me. *I will never know.*

From morning till dark, strangers filled our streets. "Look out for the crooks," my stepchildren warned. "You can be mugged or, at the least, taken advantage of as you shop." After a few years, I thought I developed an instinct about who to trust and who not to in this bustling city.

Eventually, I enjoyed the daily trip to the upper market, the haggle over prices, the smell of food and animals and people all scrunched into tiny alleys. And it was exciting to meet people from towns far and wide. Sometimes, I happened upon a vendor from Emmaus, and was thrilled to hear about life in my hometown. A few vendors became my favorites because they seemed honest and carried quality product. I learned the hard way that trust without wisdom makes one quite vulnerable. I'm not making excuses. Only I am responsible for both my good and bad actions, regardless of how naïve I might call myself.

After years of buying from the same traders, I had the most confidence in a particular man. His seeming kind interest in my family was like that of a friend. In all honesty, it felt good to have a man show interest in my life. His attention lured me into a lair I never imagined possible. I was frightened. When everyone learned the dishonor I brought to my husband and family, guilt and shame consumed me like a great wave. *Wash me away*, was my last desire.

I am well aware of the tradition: a woman caught in adultery is stoned to death. I never took part in that inhumane punishment. But I did hang around to watch. The woman's eyes filled with pain, fear and disbelief. She begged for mercy. Red-faced, angry men offered none; one by one they raised heavy stones. Fury strengthened throw after throw. The memory of those horrors always makes me shudder. *Now it's my turn.*

"Take her with us." His voice was dark. The local synagogue leader seized my arm and practically dragged me through narrow streets to the Temple. *I am probably the most immoral person who ever lived. I deserve such a horrid death.* I had one hope that my life would be spared: because of the Roman occupation, Jews needed permission for everything, including to execute a Jew who broke their own law.

A cloud of stifling dust carried me and the growing crowd to my final destination. Their remarks were like swords that pierced my heart. "Evil!" And, "Disgusting!" Or, "Immoral and dirty!" Jabs accompanied their ugly accusations. People pulled my hair, and it fell loose.

Then I was thrust headlong into the dirt at the feet of the scribes and Pharisees. "Look at this," the leader's high pitched cry could be heard for miles, I'm sure. "She has been caught in adultery!"

The dust settled around us and one by one the face of each spangled Pharisee put on the same sly smile. With arms crossed and eyebrows raised, they nodded to one another in that way that says, "We are all thinking the same wicked thought – she will never do this again." One stepped forward and grabbed my arm. He shoved me toward a crowd sitting in the outer courts. I stumbled over many sandaled feet and landed where a man sat on a mat, facing the group, as though teaching.

Then I looked up. *Oh, no! It's Jesus of Nazareth.* I had heard him teach. He seemed so different from any person I ever knew. His dark eyes were soft with compassion. His movements were purposeful, yet gentle. His words amazed hearers over and over again. I never heard of him doing or saying one unkind thing. *Of all people, why someone who seemed so pure?* I lowered my head to the ground.

Unknown to me, the Pharisees and Sadducees had been trying for days to trick Jesus into a reason to bring him to court. As a pawn in their plan, they were thrilled at my disgrace. In their minds, the timing couldn't be more perfect. They were well aware that Jesus was versed in Scripture that directed adulterers be stoned to death. But they also knew the Roman requirements. Some of them actually licked their fat lips as they wondered how Jesus would talk his way out of this one.

With a thunderous voice that feigned respect, my accuser boomed, "Teacher, this woman was seized in the very act of adultery. In our law, Moses commanded us to execute a woman like her by stoning. What do you say we should do?" He spun around to me. "Stand up, you!"

I took my time to stand, careful to keep my head low and eyes closed. *I cannot look into Jesus' eyes.* I held my breath. What will his answer be? Silence hung in the air. Finally, I raised my head just enough to peek.

Jesus leaned forward and drew in the dirt with his finger. His move incensed the religious leaders. Unable to keep quiet any longer, they badgered him with questions about my situation and their beloved law.

Lifting my head a bit more, I trembled as Jesus straightened up. One by one, he looked each man in the eye. They waited. His response astounded us all, "Let the one who is sinless among you throw the first stone at her."

A tiny gasp escaped my lips. *I am so bewildered. The sin of adultery, or any sin? Who did I know who didn't sin? Maybe only this man called Jesus. Oh, no! Does that mean he will throw the first stone? He is so kind, surely not. But I am such a sinner.* Fear strangled and choked me.

No one spoke or moved.

Jesus squatted then, and his cloak settled in the dust. Without a word, he drew in the dirt again. I stole a glimpse around. One by one the Pharisees and scribes realized the miserable failure of their trick, dropped their heads to face the ground, and shuffled out of Jesus' presence in silence. The oldest led them. Even the gawking townspeople scuffed away without a word.

This is it. Only Jesus and I are left. Now he alone will stone me to death. How could I possibly be so wrong about people's character? I misjudged the market vendor. Now, Jesus.

Still squatting, he glanced up at me. "Woman, where are your accusers? Has no one stayed to condemn you?"

My eyes traveled slowly around me. "No one, Lord," I whispered. Jumbled thoughts raced through my mind. *I can barely breathe.*

Jesus leveled his eyes at me as he pronounced each word carefully, "I don't condemn you either. Go on your way, but do not sin again."

I stood still as a stone idol. *What did I just hear? Could the gossip be true that Jesus was the long-awaited Messiah? Who else could forgive my sin?* The heavy beat of dread no longer thumped within; instead my heart quickened. Tears of gratefulness, not shame, sprang from my eyes. A smile grew that was nearly too large for my face to contain.

I dropped to my knees. I bowed my head, let tears continue to stream, and squeezed my hands together. "Thank you, Lord. Thank you. Because of you, I live. Today I choose never to sin again."

Has my life been easy since that moment of forgiveness? Of course not. Under Roman occupation, a Jew's life is not easy. Have I been perfect and sinless? Impossible. I am still human.

I spend my days trying to be more like the One who saved me. I serve not just him but those he came to save – the poor, the lonely and forgotten, the widows and orphans, the homeless, the sinners. Each day I recognize a change in my heart as joy overflows. I am more patient and, certainly, more forgiving. When I fail, I acknowledge my sin, and beg God's forgiveness again, certain to receive it. His peace covers my entire being. And that has made all the difference.

Based on the story in John 8:2-11

19 ♦ How Can I
Keep From Singing?

I wanted to obey the man who changed my life. But I was so
overjoyed, the words spilled out before I remembered not to
tell. And besides, every single person in my life knew
immediately the change that happened; it couldn't be hidden.

I nearly died from a high fever as a young child. My parents said
that after the fever left, I stopped my childish quest to know the
world around me through questions and no longer responded to
sounds. My speech patterns lessened and my vocabulary
decreased. It was so long ago that the memory of the sound of my
mother's voice, or even my own, diminished to nothingness.

I live in a vacuum. That thought haunted me. It's impossible to
describe what it was like to hear absolutely no sound. It's also
impossible to describe what it feels like to never fully participate
in the joys and sorrows, discoveries and adventures of others.
Lonely? That's a gross understatement. Afraid? Definitely.
Cautious? Always. Worthless? Usually.

When everyone around me laughed or cried and I had no idea
why, what could I do? I walked closer and stared into their faces,
tilting my head as though a new angle could help me figure out
why they were doing whatever. I'm sure my face said, "Please, let
me in on this." But even if they pointed to the person or situation
they were involved with, I couldn't share the moment. When the
neighborhood children called to each other to play a game, or
investigate a commotion down the road, I didn't hear the shouts.
So I never joined. When someone came up behind me on my way
to the market, my heart skipped a beat and I jumped when they
suddenly appeared.

My brother tried to teach me to read so I could attend synagogue
with the boys in my neighborhood. But since I couldn't hear

pronunciations, there's no telling what garbled noise came from me. People's laughter, that I could only see, crushed me. I studied the movement of their mouths as they recited what they read. *What are those sounds?* It was evident that I would never be a leader in the synagogue, let alone of my own household.

I begged alms to help with my parents' household needs. Day in and day out, in icy cold or pouring rain or scorching sun, I waved my cup by the city gates. Hopelessness covered me. *Why do I live?* Fear gripped me. *What will happen to me when my parents die?* Endless dust swirled around me and into my nostrils. It choked me more while sitting, so I wandered from place to place, staying at this gate or that building corner, until someone shooed me away and I dragged myself on. When Pharisees looked at me, squinted and then immediately pivoted themselves away from me, I wanted to crawl into a hole. Sometimes I believed what their actions insinuated: I am dirtier on the inside than the outside.

One day I searched for a new begging spot and found myself stuck in a crowd of fired-up people. I tried to wrench myself away but there were too many. I would be crushed if I stood against their strong tide.

And then, as one solid unit, they stopped. Their mouths dropped open and, on tiptoe, they stretched their necks to peer over one another. I stood on my toes, too, and craned my neck to look with them. *It's a rabbi. He must be talking to them.*

We stood still for what felt like forever to one who lives in silence.

And then the people shuffled around. One of my older brothers and his friends walked toward me. *I didn't know Judah was here. What's going on?* Judah caught my eye and waved me over to him. *It's times like this that I truly hate being deaf.* I had no choice but to go to him. The crowd opened a path for Judah to lead me right to the rabbi. *Oh, no. Am I in trouble? What have I done? Judah's my friend! Would he set me up?*

I jumped back and yanked my arm away. I opened my mouth to yell. *Useless. Whenever I'm in a panic, I tend to forget that I can't communicate with anyone.* With a firm grip, Judah took my arm and planted me, squirming, in front of the teacher with friendly eyes. Judah and his friends waved their hands around and changed their facial expressions as they talked to the rabbi. They often pointed at me. Later I learned they were telling him about my deafness and inability to speak because of it. They asked him to heal me. I'm not sure I would have stayed if I had had any idea of the conversation.

Though the man looked kind, when he drew me away from the throng of onlookers, I trembled. *I'm so thankful Judah is still with me.* And then, the rabbi placed his fingers in my ears! I wiggled to get away but Judah held me in place. And then the rabbi spat on his fingers and touched my tongue! *What's he doing to me?* He looked toward the heavens. At the very instant that his lips moved in speech, I grabbed my ears as pain shot through them. *Ouch!*

My reaction to whatever he did to me caused people around me to gasp and sing and talk all at once. *My ears are open!* My hands flew to cover my ears as their noise overpowered my newfound sense. And then I shouted, in a strong, clear voice that even I understood, "I can hear! He healed me! It's like I'm new!" Tears muddied my dirty face. I looked at the rabbi. When he smiled, all the sadness of my life to that point melted out of me and joy plunged deep into my heart. He began to turn back to the people, but I grabbed his arm, "Who are you?"

"I am Jesus of Nazareth."

"Jesus of Nazareth," I repeated in a dazed whisper. "Thank you. Thank you!"

Before he returned to the now enormous group, he smiled once more. Then he locked his eyes on mine, and in a quiet voice said slowly and deliberately, "Tell no one."

I looked at Judah. He sniffled a red nose on his wet face. His great stone mason arms enveloped me. We rocked together and wept.

Such a life changing memory. I learned to read and became a leader in the synagogue. I apprenticed with my brothers and earned a wage to help my parents' household. Somehow I hoped to make up for their years of sacrifice because of me. Eventually I married; we have five children.

Everywhere I go, I tell the story of the teacher, Jesus of Nazareth, who will change the life of anyone who approaches him, even if they don't know him.

May God have all the glory!

Based on the story in Mark 7:31-37

20 ✦ I Chose Joy

Mary and I are as different as Spring and Fall.

Mary is a dreamer. Many afternoons I find her gazing at the sky with untouched mending in her lap. She sits in the background while people discuss the mysteries of life, and her sparkling eyes tell everyone she's enthralled. She always pays attention at synagogue.

Then, there's me. I find sitting for any length of time an agony. I'm antsy unless I'm moving and doing something. If I can mend clothing or make bread at the same time, I can listen to a discussion. Every minute must count. Time spent at synagogue used to be torture. I tried to focus on the readings and prayers, but my mind constantly brought me to my To Do List. In fact, Sabbath itself was extra difficult because I wasn't allowed to work!

It didn't really bother me that Mary and I don't quite equally share household responsibilities. In fact, I often envied her. She was aware of the need to feed an internal longing and kept that separate from the physical needs of life around her. So, if tending that longing inside kept her from getting things done, she didn't mind. Besides, to take care of the house and make it a welcome place for visitors energizes me. Serving guests gives me great pleasure.

Of course, one of our favorite guests is Jesus, a good friend of our brother Lazarus. He's quite interesting, and filled with wisdom that I never heard from any man. Even I like to pause to listen when he talks. When we have notice that he's coming, we prepare as fully as possible beforehand. That way I, too, can stop to soak in his brilliance.

My mind still can't grasp what possessed me the day he put me in my place.

One of Jesus' friends ran ahead to tell us they were headed our way. Naturally, I keep my house clean and in order, so I wasn't concerned in that area. But there are several special foods I like to offer guests, which made the afternoon hectic. Mary and I partnered well in times like that and I was grateful for her.

We were nearly ready when I heard Lazarus, "Welcome, my dear friend. It is so good to see you, as always." I turned to see them embrace; Jesus smiled at me over Lazarus' shoulder.

I wiped my hands and set down my towel, then hurried to greet Jesus. Already, I was not focused. *Oh, if I had just one more hour.* As I embraced him, I looked beyond him to many more than the usual number of friends in tow. *Oh, no.* "Come in, come in. Welcome to our home." My bright smile didn't match my thoughts. *I hope he doesn't sense my tension.*

As people piled in, Mary and I moved deftly to set out food and drinks and to make sure everyone was comfortable. As much as I love these events, that day I felt harried.

At last the men settled in. They ate, they drank, they talked and laughed. I began to relax. *There's still a lot to do to keep the afternoon running smoothly, but I finally feel like we can manage.*

Eventually, the inevitable question came up that required intense listening as Jesus shared from a soul that seems to know everything there is to know. *I wish I could sit and listen but there are just too many people for relaxation.* As I scurried about, I began to feel like I was missing an arm. *I can't keep up with the re-filling of plates and drinks.* My chest began to tighten. But when I saw my lovely sister sitting at the feet of Jesus, listening and not helping, my head began to ache and my hands began to shake. *No wonder I'm so stressed. I'm doing this all alone. Oh, Mary, even this day you must stop working?*

With my stomach in knots, I continued. I reminded myself to smile. *What kind of a hostess am I?* And then I dropped a bowl of hummus. *That's it. I have to say something.*

With more boldness than propriety permitted, I walked up to Jesus. Tapping my foot lightly, I waited for a break in the discussion. Finally, I had a chance to blurt, "Lord, don't you care that my sister has left me to serve all alone? Please tell her to help me." I let go a long, deep breath.

And then my Lord gently put me in my place. "Martha, Martha you are worried and upset about so many things. Only one thing is really necessary. Mary has chosen the better part. She chose joy. It will not be taken away from her."

The heat in my face told me that our gathered guests saw my embarrassment. My eyes filled to the brim. I sank to the floor by his side. "Oh, Lord, please forgive me. Of course. Your words are those of everlasting life. My household chores are here today and gone tomorrow." He smiled tenderly and stroked my head. I was forgiven.

In silence, I sat and pondered his words. *Only one thing is necessary – pure joy. It can't be taken away.* The words went round and round in my head like a wheel on an out-of-control cart rolling downhill. I closed my eyes and intentionally breathed slowly. When he speaks, the very air in the room is life. His words reached my soul more deeply than ever. *Why am I so affected by his teaching this time? I know exactly why - because I usually let my mind and my To Do List cover the ears of my heart.*

I felt a spark of Mary's choice to focus on his words whenever he is near. *As an unmarried woman with few talents, it's an honor to have a friend like him. Why would I ever want to squander any chance to let his truth pierce my heart? I want joy, too – through the words of everlasting life that can only come from the heart of God. Let them feed my soul that I may change and live forever.*

Now, when I allow my heart to listen, I can balance my priorities. Yes, housekeeping and hospitality are wonderful gifts. But only in this life. Today I yearn for what can never be taken away and I will do whatever I must to have it, regardless of the chores to be done around me. For all of my days, I am humbly thankful.

Based on the story in Luke 10:38-42

21 ✦ Love Found Me

S weat trickled down my body under my tunic as I headed to the well for the third time that summer day. I drew up the heavy bucket, then suddenly dropped it and fell to the ground with an anguished scream that reached the cloudless sky. Excruciating pain pierced my back.

I'm alone. And I can't get up. I'm like a brick baking in the sun. When will someone find me? A million thoughts jumbled through my head, as pain racked my entire body that lay curled like a baby. Tears squeezed out of my eyes, shut tight against the brilliant light that covered me. *What if no one comes till dark and a lion roams near?* I was afraid.

After what seemed an eternity, Mother sent a younger brother to find me. He ran home crying for help.

That night a raging fever entered my body that lasted weeks. I saw strange shapes and heard loud voices inside my head. I didn't know where I was. I couldn't eat or drink. Finally, after every known medical and herbal remedy was administered, the fever melted away from my wasted body. Its damage remained: I dragged one leg and limped on the other; I leaned bent over on a thick branch made into a walking stick. My energy was drained by mid morning each day. In a flash, eighteen years ago my life changed from vibrant and strong to dull and battered.

I can't blame Neriah, soon to be my betrothed, for rejecting me. What good would a crippled wife be to a young man ready to start a family? I became a burden to everyone, the greatest to my mother who had four younger children. I moved to my married sister's home to lighten the load for Mother. Leaving her added to the sadness that oozed into every crevice of my heart.

I hobbled and helped as much as possible. My sister's family tried to include me in their life. But my back never straightened, keeping me an oddity. And the pain never ceased, making it almost impossible to enjoy anything. A constant thought disturbed me: *This is what hell must be like.*

Because our village sat by beautiful Lake Samachonitis, north of the Galilee, we received travelers often. One day several visitors arrived who had a rabbi in their company. He taught at synagogue the day after they arrived.

His brilliant understanding of Scripture mesmerized us. His words enlightened our souls like the morning sun fills a new day. His name was Jesus of Nazareth.

Whispers filled the air as we headed out of the synagogue. "Who is that man?" Or, "No one has ever taught like that before. His words gave me chills." And, "I couldn't take my eyes off his face."

Just as we women approached the courtyard, that magnificent voice called out, "Woman, you are freed from your affliction."

I think he's talking to me! I shuffled to turn toward him and twisted my head sideways to look up. He approached swiftly and laid his hands on my head.

In that instant I knew what it felt like when sunlight dances on water as the wind ripples across it. The sensation coursed throughout my entire body. Without an ounce of effort, or being held back by pain, I stood upright. And without thinking, I raised my arms and praised my God with a loud voice.

Family and friends gushed toward me. They cried, they laughed, they hugged me. We danced together. *I'm dancing!*

As I tried to grasp the gift just given to me, the indignant voice of our synagogue ruler admonished us, "There are six days to get your work done. Come on one of those days if you need healing. Don't come to be healed on the Sabbath."

What? God only heals six days a week? He would hold back a gift because it's work? Besides, I didn't even come here today for healing.

Before I had a chance to defend my restored body, Jesus answered for me, "You hypocrites! You untie your ox and get your donkey from his stall each Sabbath and lead them to water. This woman is a daughter of Abraham, but Satan has kept her in bondage for eighteen long years. Isn't it right to set her free on the Sabbath day?"

Each leader was shamed into silence.

My head spun. *Satan did this to me? How did Jesus know I've been disabled for 18 years? He called me a daughter of Abraham – I've never known such respect!*

"Thank you! Thank you!" was my only response to their argument as I continued to spin in a dance.

From that day I have believed in the man who gave me life without my asking, who healed me without asking for payment. I believe in the man who chose me out of many at synagogue that day, for no reason I can imagine. He chose me, a woman. I believe in the man who knew me before I knew him. I have no idea how he healed me. But I've learned that is his way. He heals in ways we can't understand and changes lives of all people because he loves. Today I do my best to love like Jesus.

Based on the story in Luke 13:10

22 ♦ I Became A Giver, Too

"A bijah!" one of my father's friends ran into our courtyard, out of breath. "He's coming this way." *Who's coming this way? What's he talking about?*

My father's face lit up. "Where?" His eyes scanned the road. *Well, he knows.*

"He's headed into the hills on the north side." More friends gathered round. They all chattered at once.

A few minutes later Mother stepped outside, wiping her hands on a towel. "What's going on?"

Father called over his friends' excited voices, "Jesus from Nazareth is nearby. They said thousands of people are following him."

"Will you also go?" She inched her way to the men clustered by Father.

"Yes, Ruth, I will. In fact, the boys are old enough to go, as well."

"Not Jehiel?" her eyes fell on me as she spoke.

"Yes, Ruth. He is old enough. I'll look out for him. Don't worry."

A huge smile spread across my face. I didn't know where we were headed but it sure sounded like a treat to a nine year old.

My mother used to tell me that the people in Bethsaida lived better than those in many towns. Fishing was a very profitable business and involved many people besides fishermen. Blacksmiths made the fishing weights. The potter made containers to ship fresh or dried fish to Jerusalem or other cities in the empire because everyone loved the fish of the Galilee. Of course, carpenters built the boats.

I didn't understand what she meant about us living better than anyone. It all seemed normal to me. Our home had a room on the second floor where I slept with my four brothers and sisters. We had a separate kitchen and a courtyard, too. We even had a wine cellar that provided refreshing escape on the hottest days. At our house there were always plenty of olives, flat bread, pomegranates, citron and figs. And, of course, fish. Years later I realized how blessed we were.

Bethsaida was known for its mild and healing climate. Still, as a fishing town on the Galilee, it often experienced powerful storms that rolled in off the lake, with little or no warning. I didn't mind the storms. I was young enough to think the storms were adventurous!

My father was a fisherman. He didn't share my opinion of sudden violent weather changes because he worked hard through the night when the storms were most frightening. He said night fishing was best because the fish couldn't see his great net. Even though I sometimes wished he were home at night, I was lucky to have my father around during most daylight hours. If he were a day laborer who worked long hard hours, he'd have little energy in the evenings for us. In fact, it was because his days were free that we became part of an amazing event. Father had just woken up and eaten when his fisherman friends stopped by with the news.

We took the skins and sacks that Mother prepared and took off. Baking in the sun, shoulder to shoulder with family, friends and strangers, we traveled as one body to find the man called Jesus. *There are more people here than just from Bethsaida. I'll bet they've come from neighboring villages.* Later, someone said there were at least 5,000 of us crammed together on that hillside, not counting women and children.

Father made sure I stayed close by. I was kind of afraid of getting lost. Or crushed. He said my ten and twelve year old brothers were old enough to take care of themselves. *I hope so!* I kept my neck craned in search of them.

We listened to story after story. Like morning fog that covers the sea, silence enveloped us as Jesus spoke.

How is he able to speak for everyone to hear? Yet, he's not yelling. Eyes lit up as they fastened on his eyes. I only understood some of his stories, like the ones about God wanting us to forgive people who hurt us. Or the stories about helping people who have less than we do.

But the great stories didn't compare to the healings. All day, people lined up waiting to be healed. A crippled man carried to Jesus bounded away on his own two feet. People pale with fevers who could barely hold themselves up looked refreshed after his touch. Every deaf person ran off singing about the voice of Jesus. The blind people stood for several minutes blinking and smiling at us until they burst into tears and skipped away.

The day stretched on. My wineskin was just about empty. My stomach told me it was meal time. The people around me whispered that they were hungry. It didn't look like anyone had brought much, if any, food. *I am so thankful for my mother.* I recalled my parents' conversation before we left.

"Ruth, we only need a little wine mixed with water. We won't be gone long. You'll see."

"You'll see," my mother repeated. She shook her head slowly from side to side as her hands quickly wrapped up fish and bread. "You never know how long a day can be. Is there a problem with being prepared for the unseen?"

"No, I'm sure there's not," said Father. He gave in to her.

"Good," Mother said with a smug smile as she packed a sack with five barley loaves and two fish, then handed it to me. We each carried a skin of wine and water. *Was she the only person who thought ahead like that?*

We were at the front of the crowd and overheard Jesus ask one of his friends, "Where can we buy food for all these people so they can eat?" *What? He wants to buy enough to feed everyone?*

His friend shared my sentiment, "A year's wages wouldn't buy enough for each of them to get a little, let alone satisfy all of them."

His friends started walking through the crowd and asked, "Who has food to share? Does anyone have food they can share?"

"Perhaps we can gather all the food and share it among us. Bring us your food," they pleaded.

The man called Andrew stood near me. I looked up at Father who nodded, okay.

"Excuse me, sir. Yes, I have a little food here. I can help."

When Andrew bent down toward me, he smelled of the sea. *A fisherman, like Father.* "Thank you, son."

The men begged for food through the hungry crowd who began to grumble. It seemed everyone suddenly realized how far from home they had traveled and that they were now hot and hungry.

Jesus had been quietly healing people while his friends searched for sustenance. He glanced up as another child happily skipped away. The men walked up at the same time. "Well? What did you find, Andrew?"

"Teacher, from all these people, we've only gathered five barley loaves and two fishes from a boy over there." Andrew pointed toward me; Jesus' eyes followed Andrew's hand and fixed on mine. I couldn't lower my eyes, even though I should have been more respectful.

In a quiet voice, Jesus instructed Andrew, "Bring them here. Make the people sit down."

Andrew gave him my food, then he and his friends directed us to sit down by lifting their arms out with palms up, and lowering them, palms down. Like rolling waves on the Galilee, row after endless row of sweaty people sat or squatted.

What happened next was beyond anyone's imagination. I am certain if I hadn't been there myself, I might have said it was a lie or a dream.

When we were all settled, Jesus held up my barley loaves and fish to the heavens. Then he gave thanks to his father. *He's thanking his father? Is his father nearby?* Next, he broke the bread and the fish and handed it to his friends with instructions to feed everyone. *Does he really think this is going to work?*

I kept an eye on my meager contribution. It seemed there was always bread or fish in his hands to break and give away. I watched every step. His friends held their arms to gather the pieces from him. They handed it all out and returned for more. Some people gave baskets to the disciples to speed up the process. The baskets were filled and sent into the crowd to take as much as needed. Empty baskets returned, refilled, were sent out again. I lost track of how often.

No one talked - not even the children. We focused on the miracle all around us. My dazed eyes stayed on Jesus' hands. He remained calm and broke piece after piece. Every now and then, I glanced up at Father. His face never left that of Jesus. We ate until every belly was full.

By the time our hunger was satisfied, the sun had circled to the stainless western sky. And when Jesus' companions handed him twelve baskets filled with leftovers, the spell seemed to break.

Without a command, the body of fed men rose and shouted with one voice, "This is the prophet foretold by Moses. Let's make him king!"

The King of the Jews! I'm in the presence of the King of the Jews? I wanted to shout with them and jump around. Instead, I clenched my father's cloak because the crowd riled up more. *This is scary.*

I tried to keep my eye on both Father and Jesus. People angrily elbowed each other toward Jesus. I lost sight of him. A line of men walked toward the sea. *That's him and his disciples.* The crowd shifted direction. His friends entered boats. Jesus stood on the shore, staring at the people as they closed in on him.

It was then I heard my name over the pandemonium, "Jehiel! Listen to me!"

"Oh, Father, I'm sorry. I wanted to watch Jesus."

"Here are your brothers. Let's go. Now!"

I can't wait to tell Mother what happened today!

That was a very long time ago. I mentioned how well we lived in Bethsaida. After my father encountered Jesus, he was not the same. From that day till now, he makes certain that every person he comes into contact with has food and shelter. If they don't, he takes care of the need himself or helps that person get what they lack.

Because of the new model of giving in our family, my life now, as a fisherman with my own family, is centered around giving, not gathering. I am content because I have learned to give thanks in all things, even though some times may be bleak. God will take care of his own, and that includes me.

Based on the stories in Matthew 14:13-22, Mark 6:30-45, Luke 9:10-17, and John 6:1-13

23 ♦ So Much Faith

I t's a ghost!" we cried out together. Our eyes were wide as we clung to each other or the boat – anything we were close to – as though we could be safe that way.

I'll never forget that night. We were all exhausted. First, our emotions were battered with the news that Herod beheaded Jesus' cousin John the Baptizer. A long day of Jesus' teaching followed. It didn't matter how much he needed alone time or where he tried to hide, people found him. Thousands gathered round him in a wide open space. He performed incredulous healings throughout the day of teaching. The day ended with a magnificent miracle where a mere five loaves and two fishes fed every single person present – with baskets of food leftover! Jesus saw how overwhelmed we were, so he sent us ahead to begin our journey across the sea. He said he'd wrap up the teaching and the healings, then send the people home. *He has more stamina than any man I've ever known.*

Our conversation bubbled as we descended to the shore. Excitement seemed to filter through the salt air and revitalize us to push off. Eventually, we settled into quiet talk with thoughtful pauses until all but the watchmen drifted into heavy, contented sleep.

About seven hours into the night – the fourth watch –super-powered winds surprised us and stirred up monstrous waves. It doesn't matter how many years men have fished and traveled that sea, everyone feels at least a bit of fear each time he experiences the changing Sea of Galilee.

We sprang out of sleep and ran to our stations. *This is it. I can't remember when it's been so bad out here. We are really in trouble.*

And just as I had those thoughts, one of the crew called out above the storm's noise, "Look!"

We all shielded our eyes from the downpour and gazed out toward the horizon. Our voices rose together, "It's a ghost!"

I can't explain the anxiety and fear that gripped me. My heart pounded wildly with the dread of impending death. I gasped through a sense of strangulation. Then, a loud voice, yet soothing, called over the storm, "Cheer up. It is I." *Is that Jesus? How is that possible?*

Then Peter, ever our leader when Jesus was not around, spoke, "Lord, if it really is you, call me to come join you on the water."

Immediately Jesus replied, "Come."

Peter instantly obeyed and stepped out of the boat. *Peter! What are you doing? Are you crazy?*

He proceeded to walk right on top of the water. He kept his eyes on the face of Jesus, his goal. I held my breath as I squinted through the torrential rain and waves that beat my face. And then it occurred to me. *Peter's not crazy. He actually has faith that I don't.*

Just before he reached Jesus, the wind gusted about 30 knots. Peter glanced around at the growling waves and in that second when he took his eyes off Jesus, he began to sink. *Peter, no!*

He flailed his arms toward Jesus, "Lord, save me!"

Jesus, standing amazingly still in the midst of the raging storm, reached out and took one of Peter's hands. He lifted him up and held him in his arms. As Jesus carried Peter to the boat where we stood in awe, he looked into Peter's face and with an aching voice said, "Your faith is so small. Why did you doubt?"

When they stepped into the boat, the wind abruptly ceased. The sea became like glass so that the bright moon reflected in it again. Without a word, each of us on board fell to our knees and placed our foreheads on the ship's bottom. We worshipped the Lord who saves, the One we now professed as the Son of God.

From that night, my heart burned to know faith like Peter. Of us all, only he believed – and proved – that if we keep our eyes on Jesus, all will be well.

Based on the story in Matthew 14:22

24 ✦ Restored

I don't care what they think or what they might do. A woman. A Canaanite woman, no less. Approaching a Rabbi. But this is about my daughter and I will do whatever it takes for her. It amazed me how many Jews couldn't see that he was Israel's long-awaited Messiah. Who else could cast out demons, heal the sick, and make the blind to see? *Interesting that he came to our town full of Gentiles.* I made my way quickly through the streets. News of a Jew entering Tyre travels fast. This one and his friends are known far and wide. *I'm sure I can find them.*

While I raced from street to street, I recalled with vividness the day Diana was born. *The midwife said she had never delivered such a tiny baby with such glowing health.* From that moment, Diana amazed us with beauty and health, as well as a sweetness unlike my other children. She was a content baby who rarely cried. As she grew up, she pitched in to help with chores before I asked. Diana became known as 'the smiling helper' in our neighborhood. If I wondered where she wandered off to, I'd find her helping a neighbor with a distraught infant or a bored two year old. Everyone delighted in her.

There, I see a group of men with a rabbi. I stepped up my pace. When I got closer I started calling out, "Help me, Lord!"

His friends looked at me in disgust. "Shall we send her away?" they asked the teacher. "She keeps screeching at us like a mad bird."

"If I had not been sent, what would become of those who are dying everywhere, especially in the house of Israel?" he turned to me with compassion even though his words were meant to send me away.

In my mind's eye, I saw ten year old Diana, shrieking, her eyes glazed and face twisted. *What has happened to her? Two agonizing years of violent outbursts, cruel speech, and flailing actions.* The full impact of my purpose overtook me. With tears streaming, I ran to Jesus and threw myself at his feet.

"My daughter is possessed by an unclean spirit." I lowered my eyes and begged, "Lord, help me." I raised my eyes to his. *Kindness mixed with agony in deep-set eyes.*

"Is it right and beautiful to take bread that was meant for the children and toss it to their puppies?"

I know we're nothing but little mongrels to the Jews. After all, look at our history. Maybe this is a test. He might wonder what kind of Canaanite I might be. Regardless of his reason, he can't offend me. And I won't be refused; my daughter's life is at stake. I don't care that he was sent to the House of Israel first. I won't give up.

"Yes, Lord, but even the dogs eat the crumbs that fall from their master's table." *This man is master of all. He is the longed-for Redeemer. No man of his integrity can say no to a child in need.*

He half-smiled, raised his eyebrows, and peered at me. *He must be amazed at my boldness.*

And like morning dew renews the fields, his words fell on my ears and renewed my strength, "Dear woman, you have a great deal of faith. It will happen just as you wish it."

"Thank you, thank you, Lord. I will praise you forever. Thank you!" Tears of joy sprang from my eyes and blurred my vision.

He continued on his way and I took off in the other direction. Thoughts jumbled through my mind. *Who am I to this Rabbi? I'm a stranger, a Gentile woman. I am no one. Yet he spoke to me with the same respect he would give any Jew.* With the deftness of a horse racing to the finish line, I made it home.

There in the garden are my children and my husband. My sister and her children are here, as well. Why is everyone talking at once? My heartbeat quickened. My husband spotted me first and ran to meet me. I searched his eyes and face for an answer. Before I could speak, he yanked my hand and practically dragged me to the house.

"Sophia! Hurry! Come see Diana!" Dimitrius and I hurried past our chattering friends and relatives to the doorway.

And there she stood. "My Diana," I whispered. Rapid-fire thoughts raced through my mind. *Her hair is neat and shiny. Her face is glowing. Her round brown eyes sparkle above her beautiful smile.* In unison she and I cried out to each other. Tears cascaded down my face as I swept her into my arms. "Oh, my child. You are healed! Praise be to the Lord, the Son of David!"

"Mother, it's true. I am well." Diana's skinny arms squeezed me tight around my neck. "Oh, Mother, I hated my behavior. I watched myself be rude and disobedient, but I couldn't stop. Suddenly, while you were gone, I stood up straight and tall again. In a loud voice I said, "Praise to the Son of David.""

I sang as I took her hands and we danced.

How did that day change my life? As a Gentile woman treated with dignity, I was encouraged. But more than that, my family and I found our Redeemer. In Him, we discovered life.

Diana is now a lovely woman – on the inside and in outward appearance. She is a follower of Jesus, and joyfully spreads his good news of new life to everyone she meets.

Based on the stories in Matthew 15:25-28 and Mark 7:24-30

25 ✦ Thankful For One Greater Than An Angel

D ust clung to my clammy body. Beads of moisture dripped from my hair. My back ached and one leg tingled. My hand was too tired to jiggle my wooden cup, my voice too weak to spread the word that yet another beggar was nearby, baking in the sun.

When will it end? Swarms of sweaty, stinky people suffocated me. Garments of soft linen and rough wool rubbed against my face when they shoved at each other through the gate. *They don't notice and they don't care.* I fought jealousy as they talked among themselves and seemed to glide from place to place. I wrestled with envy when the aroma of their clothing smelled of the sea, fresh cut wood, or the earth of the farm. They were reminders of places far beyond the gate that someone who was a fixture from sunrise to sunset since childhood would never experience.

The Temple is more crowded today than ever. When I focused on the noise around me, I learned that Jesus of Nazareth was inside. *What a character. People either loved him or hated him. Only he seems bold enough to stand up to the Pharisees about their endless list of rules and regulations. That alone makes me want to meet him. I mean, I find the Pharisees quite peculiar. Their lists don't always seem to match how they act. And, as far as I can tell, they're not particularly kind. But there are other things about this Jesus that I'm curious about. For one, they say he explains Scripture like no other teacher. And he heals people of serious diseases. I even heard that he casts out demons. The craziest rumor is that he's the long-awaited Messiah. That makes me imagine all kinds of things. Oh, if I could just meet him someday. Then again, if he really is a king, what are the chances of a low life like me even getting close to him?*

"Poor. Poor. Alms for the poor." *There are so many people today I can make a lot of money. I have to find energy to work, no matter how drained I am..*

From my post I heard a commotion inside the Temple. *Those loud, angry voices that are throwing out questions definitely belong to Pharisees.* But when they paused for answers, I had to strain to hear.

Next, I felt the crowd in front of me open up, as if to allow someone to pass through, while their murmurs rose. *Must be someone important.* I felt a group of people enter the opened space. They stepped in closer and stopped right in front of me. An unusual sense of peace washed over me.

"Alms. Alms for the poor." It was all I knew to say when people were near.

I heard a gruff voice from a man whose clothes smelled of the sea. "Teacher, whose sin caused this man to be born blind? Could he have sinned before he was born? Or did his parents sin, and that is why he was born blind?" *They're talking about me!*

Silence fell. I could barely breathe as everyone waited for the answer.

"He wasn't born blind because of anyone's sin. But now, God's work is clearly seen in him."

I don't know that voice. Which teacher is he? I was so confused about who he was and why they talked about me in the first place that I only picked up a few things he said. *I don't understand most of what he's talking about. But I do know the word sin. All my life the teachers and rulers said my blindness was punishment for sin. To this day, my parents weep at the thought they somehow gave me this affliction.*

And then I heard, "As long as I'm in the world, I am the world's light."

I've been told about light. I'm pretty sure I don't know what it is. When people say the sun makes light, all I can think is that it's warm. But I'm certain no man ever claimed to be light. I sensed his face close to mine. *Does he want to see behind my blindness? How strange. It sounds like he's bending over.* I heard him spit. *What's he doing now?*

And before I had another thought, I felt large hands take my face and gently turn it. *These are the hands of that rabbi.* He placed them on my eyes. In those hands was something moist that smelled like the earth.

People around me gasped. I heard sharp comments like, "What is going on? Is that mud?" And the incredulous, "What is Jesus doing?"

This rabbi is Jesus! Oh, what could this mean? Instantly, I remembered a story that my parents loved to tell me. A man named Tobit went blind while he slept under a tree where birds nested. He was blind for four years. One day the angel Raphael visited. He made a paste of fish gall and anointed Tobit's eyes. Raphael peeled away the white scales from Tobit's eyes and he could see again. They told me that story because every day they prayed that an angel would give me sight, too.

My heart skipped a beat with hope. *Is Jesus an angel? But I've been blind since birth. Never in all of history had someone born blind been made to see. But if he's an angel…*His words broke through my thoughts.

Tenderly, like a parent to a child, he said, "Go wash in the pool of Siloam." And though I didn't know this man, I obeyed his quiet command.

The pool of Siloam was a few feet away. *I know the worn path by heart. I don't need my sight to find it.* I elbowed my way through the throngs of people. My hands found the cold stone side of the pool. I knelt and leaned in, supported by the stone. I dipped my cupped hands into the cool water. With a touch of fear, I splashed the water on my face and into my eyes. Not once, but twice.

I blinked. I bent into the pool to wash my face again. I blinked. *What is this?* I stretched out my hand to touch this something in front of me. *This is the water.* I felt confused. I raised up my head. I blinked over and over. *I can see! This is what it means to see. Now I understand what people have tried to tell me forever. It never made sense.* I glanced back to the healing water, the first thing my eyes had ever seen. Then I looked around. The voices around me were from people dressed in colorful fabrics. People had always tried to explain colors and faces and the sky. For the first time, everything was real and made sense. I raced back to find Jesus.

People started shouting. They grabbed me, spun me around, and looked into my face. "Who is this?" some cried. I recognized the voices of my neighbors.

"Isn't this the man who used to sit and beg?" Some said, yes. Others disagreed.

Compelled to stop and answer them, even though I wanted to reach Jesus as fast as possible, I finally said, "Yes, it's me. I'm the man."

"But, your eyes are open! How did that happen?"

"The man named Jesus made some mud. He spread it over my eyes and told me to wash in the pool of Siloam. So, I went and washed in the water. Then suddenly I could see."

"Where is he?" They were more interested in Jesus than me.

I scanned the place where I had spent years. Nobody looked like who I imagined might be Jesus. People passed in and out of the gate. "I have no idea."

The interrogating crowd determined to take me back to the gate. They practically carried me along.

When we reached the gate, I lifted my eyes. *I had no idea that I've been sitting by such beauty. And what is beauty? All my life beauty was in the birds' song, and in the wind that cooled my scorched skin. Now beauty is so much more. I can take hold of beauty through my eyes, and store it as a picture in my heart.*

As I considered the gate, I didn't pay attention to where they took me. The colorful crowd opened and I found myself in front of a small group of men who wore shawls that matched the sky I had just seen for the first time. The shawls had fringe tied in knots in a color similar to the sky but darker. *These are the tassels I've felt as they swished past me.* The men wore little round coverings on their heads. Large boxes were strapped on their foreheads. *These men are the Pharisees?*

"Here he is. The man born blind. Now he can see." *Why is everyone angry? Maybe the Pharisees will be happy for me.*

I stumbled when someone shoved me forward.

A tall man with broad shoulders and a long beard leaned over me with cold, dark eyes. He lowered his voice as he emphasized each word, "How did you receive your sight?"

"He put mud in my eyes. I washed. Now, I see." *Why doesn't everyone share my joy that bubbles up from the depths of my soul? Is it me they're angry with? What did I do wrong?*

In a few minutes I discovered the reason for all the anxiety. It was the Sabbath. Tradition, or maybe the Law, dictated that no lifting of things or work of any kind be done on the Sabbath. *Even the work of healing, I guess. Well, they're not taking away my joy. And they can't take away my sight.*

Back and forth they argued. Everyone knew that only God could heal. But some declared that since the healing happened on a

Sabbath, it couldn't possibly have come from God. *What do they think? That even the Creator can't change the rules to work on the Sabbath if he wants to?* Some people muttered agreement with my thoughts.

Another Pharisee stepped forward. "You're the one whose eyes he opened. What's your opinion of him?"

What can I say? Until today, I only heard rumors about him. I mean, I just met him. Well, I know he's not common, that's for sure.

"He's a prophet." It was the best I could think of in the moment.

Incredibly, they decided to search for my parents to verify my being born blind. My mother and father wept when they saw me and rushed to gather me into their arms. They hesitated before letting go and I took a second to stare at their faces for the first time.

They questioned my parents relentlessly.

"Of course we know this is our son. Yes, he was born blind. Now he can see, but we don't know how. Ask him yourselves. He's an adult. He can speak for himself." It was their final answer.

Anyone who admitted a healing by Jesus could make our leaders think they believed that he was The Christ. Perhaps my parents were afraid. If they admitted that he was The Christ, before our leaders agreed to such a claim, they would be put out of the synagogue, forever. I understood.

The Pharisees made an about face to glare at me. *Here comes my turn again.* But this time their questions were different. "Give glory to God. We know that this man, Jesus, is a sinner."

I sighed. *Their inquisition and doubt weary me.* "I don't know if he's a sinner or not. What I do know is that I was blind, and now I can see."

My answer did not satisfy. They asked again how this happened. With boldness new to me, I faced them, "I told you already, but you weren't listening. Why do you want me to repeat it? Do you want to follow him and become his disciples?" I knew my response would irritate them to no end. But I was so astonished at everything I was seeing, putting faces to voices and matching colors in fabric with colors of the earth and trees, I was fed up with them and couldn't be bothered with their questions. They droned on and on. They wanted to figure out where this Jesus came from.

My final answer revealed my heart, "That's amazing. You're worried about where he's from? He opened my eyes. We know that God doesn't listen to the prayers of sinners. But if someone truly worships God and does his will, God hears that man. Never before in all of history have the eyes of someone born blind been opened. Yet, he opened my eyes. If he was not sent by God, I would still be blind."

Out of control now, they barked together, "How dare you presume to teach us! You are a sinner and have been a sinner since the day you were born." They told me to leave the synagogue, permanently.

I don't care. The man who healed me, Jesus, said my blindness had nothing to do with sin. I believe him.

Not long after, Jesus heard that I had been sent away and looked for me. "Do you believe in the Son of Man?" he asked when he found me.

"Who is he, lord, that I may believe in him?" *I'm still not completely sure. This is my first time to lay open eyes on this Jesus. His tunic is simple and the color of the earth. He's so plain.* I looked into his dark eyes. *What I see in his eyes wasn't in the eyes of those Pharisees.* When I looked into his clear eyes I felt the peace that enveloped me when he stood by me earlier.

"You are looking at him, and he is speaking to you now."

I dropped to my knees in worship. "Lord, I believe."

From that moment until this day, each morning I gaze on the sun's pink blaze as it rises in the east. Throughout the day I notice every shade of blue in the sky, the shades of green olives and tree leaves, the difference between the rich brown of dates and the lighter brown of the dust on my feet. Before I eat any meal, my eyes savor the size and cuts and lines and grain of each piece of fruit or bread or fish. Each night, I face west as oranges and purples streak a sky whose night darkness encroaches, darkness that I no longer fear. And with each of those moments, I remember why I can see and give thanks to God. He has saved me.

Based on the story in John 9:1-41

26 ✦ An Honor And A Blessing

*L*ook *at Jesus enshrouded in a blaze of light. Who's talking with him? I think it's Moses and Elijah. Yes, it is. But they're not emblazoned in the same light. It's the Shekinah glory of God!*

At first, I agreed with Peter. "Yes, Peter, this is what we've been waiting for! Let's build three shelters." *One for Moses, one for Elijah, and one for my best friend Jesus. I'd love to make a place where they rest and live and we visit. We can even celebrate our feasts with them right here at their booths. Maybe, just maybe, there's a way to keep the glory of the moment alive to, somehow, make all the bad in the world go away.*

And as if the gift to see the Shekinah glory was not enough, a brighter cloud burst forth from the heavens and covered all of us. Every self-centered thought stopped in that second.

"This is my Son, the Chosen One whom I love. My pleasure is with him. Listen to what he says."

At the sound of his voice from the cloud, I sank to my knees, then fell face down on the mountain that trembled. "Have mercy on me!" I cried out when my heart revealed that what my mind wanted – to keep them there - was impossible.

We are in the presence of Almighty God. Jesus truly is Son of the Most High. If I had one drop of doubt left, it vanished in the light. *From this moment I will listen and do whatever he instructs. I will trust his plan.*

I grew up with Jesus in Nazareth. He, my brother and I played together and ate at each other's homes. He showed us, and the other children in the neighborhood, the real difference between good and bad. We watched him take care of a hurt child on a playing field. Sometimes we walked with him to deliver his mother's needlework to a customer. It was fun to join him when he took gifts of food to families in need because their appreciation made us happy, too. He explained scripture so that we could refer to it day to day.

For his twelfth birthday his parents hosted a grand celebration. Thirteen of us gathered. Reclining as we enjoyed a great feast after the games, we felt so grown up, especially with Jesus at the head of the table. He just belonged there. Though he shared life principles as he always did, it was with new authority. Still, he remained humble.

After the party, we spent less time together since we all began apprenticeships. John and I spent endless nights on the sea with our father, an excellent fisherman. Jesus' very talented father taught him carpentry. Still, we remained close in spirit and visited on the Sabbath when we could. In spite of new responsibilities, our friendship only strengthened. Over time, I became convinced that Jesus' destiny was far greater than any of ours. No regular man had that much knowledge and wisdom.

By the time Jesus called John and me to leave our nets and follow him, we were fairly certain he was the Redeemer of the people called Israel. We had no idea how his kingship would be accomplished, but we were ready to say goodbye to our life in Galilee and be known as disciples of the Rabbi. Our families supported us because they had watched Jesus since childhood; they knew who he was, too. Our wives willingly walked by our side in the call. They fed us and stopped us to rest when our spirits wanted to push our bodies too far.

What we learned and saw and how we changed over the next few years was nothing short of miraculous. Jesus healed the sick and made the blind to see. He stood up against those who called themselves followers of the Law yet were hypocrites. They ridiculed and humiliated him. People railed against him in anger. Through it all, he maintained peace and serene love, even for his enemies. We, in his inner circle, wanted to be like him.

After a time, he began to hint about how he would be king and also how he would suffer for his kingdom. We rarely understood the powerful meaning of his words. In fact, I'm embarrassed at the audacity of John and me to coerce our mother into asking him if we could sit at his side when he became king. It just proved we didn't grasp what his kingdom would be like, despite years of soaking up his teaching.

Only now do I realize the honor we were given on Mount Tabor. We witnessed Jesus dazzling in the Shekinah glory as the resurrected Messiah. I had shielded my eyes from the blaze of white that not only surrounded him - it actually was him. I had asked myself why Moses and Elijah were not emblazoned with the light. Now I understand that in his resurrection, the law and the prophets cease to have greatest importance. Our scriptures are fulfilled by perfect love.

He has told us that we will do even greater things in his name. The thought makes my heart flutter with excitement. But he also told us that we will be persecuted because of him. I'm not afraid. I still choose to follow the Redeemer of humanity. What greater gift has God given to man than himself? Persecuted for his namesake? I willingly and gladly surrender to him.

Based on the story in Matthew 17:1-8

27 ♦ He Set Me Free!

Why didn't we go to synagogue this week?" I asked my parents.

They glanced at each other, mirrored sad eyes, then turned to face me. Father replied, "We did, son." Then they both dropped their eyes.

Again? I don't remember going to synagogue again? What's wrong with me?

It wasn't only our Sabbath duty that I often forgot. Many times my tunic had burns on it. And so did my skin. Or I'd wake up to discover myself in drenched clothes. "How did this happen?" I'd ask.

Mother or Father would say, "You don't remember, do you?"

"No," and I'd feel odd, like I should remember. "What happened?"

"Shhh...It's all right," Mother would answer, placing her arm across my shoulders. And then she'd go back to her task at hand, my signal to end the conversation.

What's wrong with me? Why can't I remember things?

The time of my manhood approached. Confusion rather than excitement filled me. "Father, why has no beautiful young woman been chosen as my betrothed?"

His dark grey-brown eyes locked on mine, "It's not possible. I'm sorry."

"But, why?"
His head hung as he walked away. *What are they not telling me?*

Not long after that conversation, my parents sat me down and told my story. They said a demon controlled me without warning. It threw me down – into fire or water or to the ground. Then my body flailed and I foamed at the mouth.

"How long does it last?" I asked. My head hurt as my mind tried to put this incredulous picture together.

"Many minutes."

"And how often does it happen?" *Oh, please, say occasionally.*

"More frequently as you've gotten older. But, yes, since you were a young child."

"And what happens when it's over?"

"Then you pant in complete and utter exhaustion and fall into a deep sleep that lasts hours."

"No! That can't be true!"

Mother wept. Father kept his head down and refused to look at me.

My mind flooded with the pieces to my life puzzle that never fit. *Of course I have no friends! How scary it must be for kids to be around me. No wonder people whisper when I'm near. I also know why I'm tired all the time. And, maybe saddest of all, I understand why Father is tense while I apprentice with him in his wood shop. He's afraid I'll be hurt – or that I'll hurt someone else!*

That discussion was a turning point in my life. Soon, I rarely smiled or took part in conversations. I didn't even care that people snickered behind their hands when I was around. I hung my head at work and no longer hummed or whistled. A young man with no future and no hope has little reason to sing.

One morning as we ate, Mother's voice had a sharp edge as she whispered Father's name, "Abuya."

He looked up from chewing his flat bread and yogurt.

"Abuya, did you hear about the man named Jesus? He's from Nazareth. He and his followers heal people."

"What do you mean, they heal people? Are they doctors?" His voice rose. "Magicians?"

"No, no, no," Mother replied. She placed her steady hand on his arm. "This Jesus is a prophet." She kept her voice low, like she didn't want my siblings to hear. I leaned in closer. "Or even greater than a prophet from what I hear. He teaches, and he heals the blind and crippled."

"Interesting." He took another bite. "So, what of it?"

"Abuya, he heals people possessed by spirits."

Father and I both stopped eating. His head shot up, his eyebrows knit together, and he squinted his eyes at her. I held my breath.

"Do you think," she hesitated. "Do you think we should take Yudan to him?"

When they looked at my wide open eyes, I let myself breathe again.

"I will do anything for our son to be whole again," my father boomed.

Mother placed her hand on my forearm and peered at me through tears.

Not long after that historic meal, we heard that followers of Jesus were in our neighborhood. My parents arranged a private meeting. We shared a new-found emotion called hope. Hope lead to joy, which I had not known since my early childhood.

But after hours with them, our joy turned to sadness. As we trudged home, the burden of hopelessness weighed on us and slowed us down. My parents filled me in on the so-called healing session. As the men prayed energetically, the spirits returned and threw me to the floor in a rage. The men continued to pray. They encouraged my parents to remain patient. But, eventually, I fell silent to the floor, washed in sweat and drained of energy. They let us stay for hours while I recovered.

As we walked, a swarm of people in a heated argument approached and surrounded us. The argument was between Jesus' followers, whom we had just left, and the scribes. Word spread that the healing prayers didn't work for me. But, it seemed I wasn't the only person to experience no results through them. The scribes were not only angry, they were also fearful that these men were magicians who could harm the villagers. They wanted explanations.

Someone at the back of the crowd yelled over them all, "Here he is! Ask him yourselves what's going on."

We wheeled around to see four men. The one who led them, as they walked toward us, literally seemed to glow.

"Jesus!" someone called out. "Tell them we're not magicians!" *The one who glows is Jesus!*

"What are you talking about?" His voice was strong and steady. *I didn't hear that confidence in the men who prayed for me.*

My brave father stepped right into the middle of the argument, "Teacher, I brought my son to you, because a spirit controls him that robs him of the ability to speak. Whenever it takes control of him, it throws him into convulsions. He foams at the mouth and grinds his teeth. He becomes rigid like a dried and withered stalk of wheat. I asked your disciples to cast it out, but they couldn't."

The glow on Jesus' face diminished. He turned to his disciples who were on the other side of the swelling crowd. His voice boomed, "This generation has no faith. Don't you know I won't be here with you forever?" He looked at my father, "Bring him to me."

My father faced Mother and me. A little light glimmered in Father's eyes as he took our hands. The three of us walked forward to Jesus. I trembled and began to get dizzy.

Why am I afraid? That was my last thought.

My parents recounted the story later. The spirit grabbed me and convulsed me. It threw me to the ground and caused me to foam at the mouth. My parents were aghast. Jesus stayed calm. He asked my father how long I had had the condition.

Jesus asked more details about my history. Father explained and ended with, "If you can do anything, please have pity on us and help us."

"If you can!" Jesus replied indignantly. "All things are possible to one who believes!"

Father said that at the sound of those words, the realization that Jesus was not a magician or mere prophet struck his heart. The faith he has in God, he knew to have in Jesus. He cried out, "I do believe. But, please, help my unbelief!"

I asked Father what it was he didn't believe. He said that though he believed Jesus could heal me, at Jesus' words, a hint of doubt hidden inside of him reared its head. Jesus recognized it. Father didn't want anything in him to prevent my healing. He was certain Jesus would deal with the unbelief and take care of me, too. So he blurted out for help with that unbelief.

Jesus thundered to the spirit that gripped me in death, "You, mute and deaf spirit, I order you to come out of him, and never enter him again."

Mother said the incident ended almost as fast as it began. But my typical deep, panting sleep after an episode didn't occur. Instead, I remained on the ground, and didn't move a muscle. My shallow breath convinced onlookers of my death. Somehow, my parents remained hopeful.

Jesus leaned down, took my hand, and lifted me to my feet.

I blinked and smiled. *This must be how a butterfly feels who stretches out of its dark, tight cocoon, into light and new life. I wish I could fly!*

"I'm free!" I shouted.

My parents rushed forward and gathered me in their arms. "Glory to God!" they repeated over and over again. We held each other close as our tears of joy mingled.

Today I am a man with a wife and many children. I work hard with my father and brothers to provide well for my family. I have more friends than I can count. At synagogue I focus on learning about the One sent to redeem us, the One who delivered me and gave me life.

Based on the story in Mark 9:14-27

28 ♦ The Kingdom Of God Is At Hand

Why the constant sense of emptiness in my life? I love my family dearly, and I know they love me. We have shelter and food and clothing. Why do I feel incomplete? I expected great insights into myself, and changes, when I stepped into the Jordan for the Baptizer to wash away my sins. For years now, I hang on every word preached by the one the Baptizer told us was coming - Jesus. Why does the kingdom of God seem so far away when he keeps saying it's at hand? Will I ever enter, especially with all these doubts? What have I missed? My uneasiness haunted me.

My grandson Mishael charged into our courtyard one day, just as I stepped out from our house.

"Whoa!" I called to the five year old. "That's quite a dust storm!"

Immediately, his little legs halted. "Sorry, 'Ëm!" he panted the grandmother title I loved to hear.

"What's all the excitement about?"

"It's that man you like to listen to. Jesus! He's here!"

I smiled. "Well, aren't you the best to let me know?" Jesus didn't get to our town in Judea very often. "Did you see him? Is he teaching out-of-doors?"

"The Pharisees are talking to him." *Of course they are. Why do they mistrust him?* "He's near our synagogue."

Well, I'm between chores. I can take a break for a grandchild. I love when the children have a chance to be near Jesus. I squatted to eye level with Mishael, "Would you like me to take you to see him?"

"Yes! Yes!" he hugged me and then jumped up and down while a huge smile covered his young face.

I closed the door of our small cube-shaped house, checked that the fire in the brazier was low enough to leave, adjusted my headpiece, donned my coat, and took Mishael's hand. I'm sorry to admit I didn't pay attention to his chatter as we headed to our synagogue, two blocks from home. *Why do I bother to go again? Can he possibly have anything new to say?* I let the barrage of self-pity fill my mind.

In a few minutes we found them – Pharisees, residents, Jesus and his friends - jabbering. It was a common gathering when he was around.

He was answering questions about divorce. *The Pharisees – always trying to trick him into a wrong answer,* I clucked to myself. *Of course, it's true that his teaching can be both radical and in line with tradition. I guess I should give the synagogue leaders some slack. They really do want to protect us from anyone who could lead us astray. I don't know, though. My heart tells me not to fear this one.*

It was a lengthy discussion. Finally, his discourse on divorce, remarriage, and adultery ended. As usual, it left people either silent or muttering.

"Can I go to Jesus, 'Ëm?" Mishael tugged my sleeve.

"Certainly. Ask him for a blessing." *Why not?*

He asked his friend Juda to join. The boys ran to Jesus with typical childish courage.

"Jesus?" Mishael's little, yet fearless, voice came from a smiling, up-turned face.

Jesus looked down at the two young friends and smiled. "Yes?"

"Will you bless us?"

And before Jesus could answer, many children were encouraged forward by their elders who called out, "Yes, bless my child, too, please."

Jesus glanced at the parents and smiled again but, in a flash, a few of his friends placed themselves between him and the children.

"Go back to your mothers," they ordered. *How rude.*

Immediately the face of every child dropped and their arms hung, lifeless, at their sides. At the same moment, every mother and grandmother mumbled disbelief.

And right then, Jesus stepped between his friends and the children. He took the hand of my Mishael. "No." He glared at his friends. "Let the little children come to me. Don't stop them. The kingdom of God belongs to little ones like these. It's very important to understand that whoever does not embrace the kingdom of God like a child shall not enter in at all."

Jesus squatted and put wide-eyed Mishael on his knee. With his hand on my little one's head, he pronounced a blessing. He did the same for each eager child surrounding him.

Mishael ran back to me. A wide grin spanned his cute face. "Did you see, 'Ëm? He blessed me. He blessed all of us."

Yes," I smiled as I took his hand. "It was wonderful." *Without a doubt, it was wonderful.*

As everyone headed home, Mishael skipped back and forth between his friends and me, happy as a lark. The neighbor women chattered but I remained silent. *He treated each child with respect and dignity. He spoke gently and in a way each could understand. He gave each one the consideration they deserved, and did not favor one over another. And each child scampered away with newfound happiness.* It occurred to me that if we treated our children with the same gentleness and respect, perhaps they would be happier and, well, better behaved. I also considered his admonishment that the kingdom of God belongs to people who are child-like.

My thoughts continued. *More like children.* I thought about what that could mean. *Children are innocent and expect good things to come their way. They love everyone and forgive without a thought. Children want to make people happy. When they fail, their sorrow is sincere. They find satisfaction in simple pleasures. In fact, they're nearly always light-hearted and unburdened by worries or fear.* I smiled to myself as I pictured my happy grandchildren. *And they give to others with no expectation of favors in return.*

At that moment I made two decisions: I will try to approach life as a child might. And I want to treat all the people in my life with respect and dignity. I want to be more like Jesus.

Powerful change in my life began that day. Confusion no longer fills my heart. Now inner strength girds me so that I can tackle the hardships of life with renewed hope. The kingdom of God is at hand; I am a part of it.

Based on the stories in Matthew 19:13-15, Mark 10:13-16, and Luke 18:15-17

29 ✦ My Perseverance Paid Off

Imagine the blow to a boy on the cusp of manhood when, as the result of a parasitic eye infection, he is left blind. Would he feel defeated when his dreams of having a family and being prosperous were snuffed out? Would he even be angry with God who allowed such a calamity to befall a child who was taught to live a life worthy of the long-awaited redeemer? Would he feel betrayed by God?

That afflicted young man was me. And I experienced each of those feelings in varying degrees from the onset of sudden blindness and for many years.

I wallowed in self pity. I took pride in nothing and pulled back from the society that shunned me. I begrudged my new vocation of beggar, and met each day under a spirit of gloom that weighed so heavy on me that my head was always down and my shoulders always drooped. I never willingly participated in any family gatherings; I chose to sit in a corner with a scowl on my face. In fact, I contributed nothing more to them than what I 'earned' begging. I could have found ways to be of value to those who still loved me, my family. But I never gave them a thought. Because I made misery my constant companion, I alienated everyone.

I still attended synagogue with my family. It wasn't by choice but because it was what good Jews did. It was there one day, many years into my darkness, that the light of hope sparked in my heart.

As usual, I merely went through the motions of prayers and recitations. Nothing in me believed any of it. I barely heard the words anyway, even when my own mouth formed them. Instead, I let the usual rants run through my head. First, I re-visited the picture in my mind of the day we heard I would never see again.

My parents screamed. Next, in my silent reverie, real tears rushed from my eyes again. All over again, I experienced that initial horror and disbelief. And, as usual at this point in my recall, I cut off my tears and began a litany of anger against God.

On that particular day, the words of tormented Job broke through my sullen and self-centered thoughts: "As for me, I know that my Redeemer lives. And, in the end, he will arise upon the earth. Even after my life has made the circle, I shall gaze upon God with my own eyes, and the longing of my heart will be fulfilled."

My head that perpetually hung low, shot up. *Yes! I do know that my Redeemer lives. He will not fail me. He did not do this to me. He is my protector. He is the Lord who leads me beside still and safe waters.* I don't know where the thoughts came from. At the same time, somewhere inside my chest a tiny tingling tickled me. It stirred and grew until it filled every cell of my body. Job's words repeated through my head, *I shall gaze upon God with my own eyes.*

I didn't know how it would ever be possible to see God, or even if it meant that my blindness would be gone someday. I only knew, as I knew my own name, that one day my eyes would set on my Redeemer who lives, regardless of my physical condition.

"Bartimaeus!"

The stern whisper of my father snapped me to alertness. "Oh! Yes, Father?" I shifted my face toward the men as they headed outside. *How long was I dreaming? Was it a dream?*

New-found hope began to grow within me. Joy that I had not known since I was a very young child entered with it. From my parents and friends, to market vendors and those who regularly dropped coins in my begging cup, every person recognized the change in me. I often heard them whisper.

140

"What's happened to Bartimaeus?"

"He actually seems happy."

"Where is his scowl?"

I never tried to discover what that day at synagogue meant and I still had no plans for my future. I continued to beg each day. But, I started to find ways to participate in family life. I began to see that others had needs, too, and that sometimes even a blind beggar could help. No more did my mind lash out in anger to God. I smiled, and the furrowed brow I had developed eased. I sent misery packing. I found ways to make meaning of my life as it was. And soon, alongside hope and joy, peace grew within.

Then, one day, as I sat and begged by the roadside, my friends told me that Jesus of Nazareth and his friends were passing by. *It's the teacher who heals.* Without thinking, I jumped up and called in a loud voice, "Jesus, have mercy on me!" I surprised myself as the words spilled out.

People began to scold me. "Leave the teacher alone."

"Go back where you belong."

"Be silent. He'll have nothing to do with you."

Their reprimands only drove me to cry out louder. Over and over, I yelled, "Son of David, have mercy on me!" I wouldn't let him pass without at least acknowledging me, even though I still had no idea what I would say when he did.

I sensed the passing group of people stop. One voice raised above those who tried to quiet me again. "Bring that man here."

The same people who tried to hush me, now attempted to befriend me, "There, there, Bartimaeus. The teacher calls you. Be encouraged."

I threw off my cloak. "Yes! Take me to him right away!" I stretched out my arms for them to lead me.

When we stopped, I heard that same steady voice that had called for me, "What would you like me to do for you?"

"Teacher, I want to see again." I kept my arms stretched toward him.

And he replied, "Go. Your faith has made you whole."

Instantly, I threw my hands over my eyes to shield them from intense sunlight. Will I ever be able to express the ecstasy when my eyes were no longer in darkness but could suddenly see the light? There are no words. I dropped to the earth in thanks. Like sinking into a cozy warm blanket after a long day of begging in the cold, my heart warmed to the knowledge that I had met my Redeemer. He came to me in love, even when I was not worthy.

As he continued on with his friends, people rushed to me, took my arms, and stood me up. They looked into my eyes that were bright and clear, no longer cloudy. I could see their wide open eyes and incredulous looks on their faces. We grabbed hands and danced, and sang praises to God.

But I didn't dance and sing for long. A compelling and overwhelming feeling led me away from their delirium to follow Jesus.

A few days later when he entered Jerusalem, crowds waved palm branches and spread their cloaks on the ground as for a king. In fact, the people called out, "Hail, King of the Jews!" The Passover and his wicked betrayal and horrid crucifixion came and went. Crushed as when I first went blind, I wearied through my days, and wondered.

But when I saw him later in his resurrected body, I knew the words of Job had at last become my own. With my own eyes I did see God, for my Redeemer lives!

Based on the story in Mark 10:46-52

30 ✦ I Only Had To Ask

We stayed together for survival, bound by our common infirmity, wanted by no one. Outcasts.

The ethnic and cultural barriers that would have separated us didn't matter. Samaritans among Jews. Galileans with Judeans.

We were all we had: Lepers who begged and ate and slept as an odd little community in the foothills of Mount Gilboa. We lived in caves and took care of each other. We even had a little system to look out for each other so that animals didn't enter while we slept and gnaw our limbs that had lost feeling. The closest places were the Samaritan town of Ginae and the Jewish town of Beth Shan. Each day, in rain or snow or scorching heat, we walked up to ten miles to beg for food and alms in one of those towns. Whatever we were lucky to get, we shared. After all, we were the only family any of us would ever have again.

Ginae wasn't my village. I lived further into Samaria. Well, I used to live there. Until my skin turned white and ulcers spread from my hands and feet to my entire body. I was 17 when I had to leave my family and every friend I ever had. Like the incessant summer song of the cicada, I can still hear my parents' wailing and see their tear-drenched faces the day I left in my new baggy clothes that identified me to all. On that day one of our priests delivered me to the colony.

Well into my new so-called life when my disease had become most horrifying in look and odor, we started catching stories in town of a Jew named Jesus who traveled all over Judea and Galilee with a group of friends. Rumors had it that he taught scripture better than the Jews' priests. What intrigued me, and some of my comrades, were the tales of his miraculous healings. People who were blind from birth could see. Crippled beggars could walk again and get work. He even healed lepers.

"What do you think about this Jew?" I asked my closest friends more than once.

The typical conversation went like this:

"He sounds like a magician to me."

"But would a magician know Scripture so well?"

"Well, I don't know about that."

"And from what I've heard, his miracles <u>always</u> work. I've never come across a magician or healer with that kind of track record."

"Well, that's true, too."

"So?"

"So, I don't know what to think."

I began to imagine what it would be like to reintegrate into society. To hug my siblings and nieces and nephews whom I had never met. Sometimes I'd get so excited about the possibility that I'd have to slap myself into reality with a question: what are the chances that this Jew and I would come into close contact? My answer was always, slim to none, as I looked at my blistered white arms and hands with bones so broken down they flopped. And I would sigh. And continue to trudge though my days.

One day a group of us approached the gates of Ginae, and saw about twenty men gathered not too far ahead. We could tell they were Jews because they didn't wear the same short skirt under their tunic that Samaritan working men wear. It's always odd to see a Jew enter a Samaritan town. Occasionally, someone might have a real need to do business in one of our towns. Some might be travelers desperate for a place to rest. In those cases, they would overlook our animosities toward each other. It was rare than an entire entourage entered.

As they got to the town, all kinds of people rushed out to greet them, which surprised us even more. It slowed them down so much that even as we hobbled we caught up to them. Of course, we called out, "Unclean!" We kept our faces covered and stayed behind them, as required.

The travelers and residents chattered at once. And then I heard the name Jesus.

I spun around to my band of brothers. "It's that Jew named Jesus!" I couldn't contain my excitement. I imagine that not just my voice sparkled, but even my dulled eyes.

We all jabbered at once.

"Should we approach?"

"And get stoned?" the fearful voice of Zephaniah replied.

"I don't think it's a good idea," the strained voice of another.

"We're not allowed to go near clean people, remember?"

I appointed myself our leader and held up my hand for them to listen to me. "I don't care," I measured my words. "Yes, we could be chased away or even stoned. Does it matter? My life is worthless, anyway. But what if he could restore our health? If we don't go forward, we'll never know."

Many heads nodded and voices buzzed in agreement. The first real hope I had known in over a decade coursed through my body like a rushing stream after heavy rains. I felt sweat on my brow. My heartbeat quickened and my hands shook.

"Then, let's go!" I beckoned.

Some still hung back. Ten of us, slowly but boldly, approached the expanding crowd. We stopped and called out simultaneously, "Jesus, watcher over Israel, we beg for your mercy!"

I held my breath. *What will happen to us now?*

We didn't need to fear. Jesus made a purposeful about-face and let his eyes rest on each of us, from one to the next and back again. And then he spoke words that shocked and confused us, "Be on your way. Present yourselves to be examined by the priests." He returned to his friends and continued into the city with them.

Our eyes were wide as we looked at each other without a word spoken.

The silence broke with my firm word, "Let's do as he says." I threw my arms up. "What else can we do?"

"True. True," the response from all.

We split up. The Jews headed to Beth Shan and we few Samaritans entered Ginae to show our priests.

In silence we rushed through the marketplace to the other side of town. I fought the urge to pause at one of my favorite begging spots. There were so many shoppers I was sure it would be a profitable day. *No. He said to show our priests. That's what I'm doing.*

I lost track of my two friends in the busy, narrow streets. *Maybe the morning's excitement made me hungry so early. I'm famished.* Each of us always started the day with a coin just in case 'work' was slow and we needed to eat before we had a trade for food. I reached into my belt for the coin at a fig stand. As customary for people like us, I waited until all customers left then crept forward and stretched my hand toward the vendor's shelf to set down the coin. I always took care to watch my own moves. I didn't want to violate social or religious taboos.

I gasped. *My hand! My skin!* I dropped the coin, grabbed the extra wide sleeve of that arm and pulled it up. *Where are my blisters and sores?* I yanked up the other sleeve. *They're gone! My skin is smooth and clear!* I started to laugh. The shopkeeper tilted his head and squinted his eyes at me.

"Where are my sores?" the words shot forth, like I needed fast verification.

He shrugged his shoulders.

With great courage I took more time than needed to unwind my face scarf, amazed now that my hands had strength, too. He shifted from foot to foot, and glanced around with eyes big as saucers to check on who might be watching.

My own eyes asked the question.

He shook his head. "No sores." He took a step back.

I forgot my hunger and my coin, and fled to find the man who had just changed my life. *He's not where I left him!* My heart pounded in my ears as I continued to run on feet free of pain up and down street after winding street. *There he is!* I quickened my pace. *It's so easy to speed up with a body that doesn't hold me back anymore!*

Since I no longer needed to announce my unclean presence to a crowd, I wove through the people around him. *I'm actually rubbing shoulders with people. Praise God Almighty!*

As each change in my body and my restored social standing dawned in my mind, a wave of giddiness flushed over me. When I flung myself at the feet of the Jew named Jesus, a river of tears flooded my clear-skinned face. "Thank you! Thank you! Thank you!"

People pressed in to investigate the commotion. He leaned down to touch my shoulder. I tilted my face toward his. He smiled. And then he stretched out his hand to help me stand. For the first time in more than ten years I placed my hand into the hand of another. A thrill of completeness flooded me as I rose with my eyes fixed on his face. *I will forever praise and thank God for this miracle!*

When I stood, he scanned the area, as though he expected to find someone else. "Weren't there ten who were cleansed?" he asked, as he continued to peer into the faces around us. His friends mumbled yes.

"Where are the other nine? Can anyone find someone else who returned to give glory to God besides this foreigner?"

Where are they? Surely they realize the gift we've been given!

And then he looked directly into my eyes as he took my hand again. "Stand up," he encouraged. His strong arm uprooted me from the ground where I still knelt. "Continue on your journey. Your faith has saved you."

My faith? How did he know my secret hope in him? Just because I asked?

He and his friends made their way down the street. I staggered away, bewildered.

It's long years since my moment of transformation. I have a full, productive life. Family and friends love me. Eventually, I learned that The Messiah who came first to the Jews also came to the Samaritans. He healed our divisions – at least those in my heart.

My faith – that faint hope – was evident to Jesus just because I asked. I discovered that because I had that tiny mustard seed of faith and approached God with it and thanked him, he mystically drew me closer and graced me with greater faith. As the cycle goes round and round I am actually stronger to deal with life. I water my seed of faith each day as I dance and sing, "Give thanks to the Lord for he is good. His mercy endures forever!"

Based on the story in Luke 17:11-19

31 ✦ The Glory Of God Is Life

My brother's body shivered uncontrollably yet his skin was almost too hot to touch. Day and night Mary and I wrapped him in warm blankets and placed cold cloths on his head and wrists. We gave him every trusted herbal concoction. The doctor came by; we followed his directions. And we prayed.

"Mary, do you think we should call for Jesus?" I finally asked. Lazarus, wasting away before us, was near death.

Under a furrowed brow, her dark hazel eyes pierced my own. After a brief hesitation she answered, "Yes."

Immediately we sent a message to Jesus. *He knows we'd only ask him to come for a serious emergency.* We were confident our dear friend would drop everything for us.

But he didn't.

My head ached as our brother slipped from life. Endless tears cascaded as we prepared him for burial. In disbelief we began to sit shiva – the traditional seven days of mourning - with our friends.

On the fourth day, a neighbor whispered in my ear, "Martha, Jesus is coming."

Without a word, I rose and left the house. *What shall I say? This wouldn't have happened if you had shown up before now? I hope I'm not that rude.* Possible scenarios of our meeting raced through my mind as I hurried to the edge of the town.

And what were the first words out of my mouth when I saw him? "Lord, if only you had been here, my brother would not have died." *Did I really say that?* To help cover my abruptness, I added what I knew as Truth, "Even now, I know that God will give you whatever you ask."

His answer surprised me. "Your brother will rise." *Well, sure, I know Lazarus will rise in the resurrection on the last day. So will I.* I told Jesus so.

But that's not what Jesus meant. "I am the resurrection. I am the life. Whoever believes in me will live, even if he dies. Everyone who lives and believes in me will never die. Do you believe this?"

This is truly a mystery. *But, somehow, yes, I do believe.* "Yes, Lord. I believe you are The Messiah, the Son of God. You have come into the world." Speaking the words that had been hidden in my heart for so long, felt as if a heavy yoke had been lifted from my shoulders.

My feet couldn't carry me fast enough to my sister at home. I signaled for her to step aside and in a hushed voice told her, "Mary, the Teacher is here. He's calling for you."

Everyone who sat shiva followed when we left the house. They assumed we left to mourn at the tomb.

We met Jesus as he approached; Mary cried and fell at his feet. She echoed my earlier agony, "Lord, if only you had been here, my brother would not have died."

Faced with heartbroken Mary and those who wept beside her, he was visibly troubled. Tears escaped Jesus' soft eyes. He asked where we had laid Lazarus.

Doubters began to murmur as we led the way to Lazarus' tomb. "This Jesus opened the eyes of the blind." And, "We've heard all the magnificent stories. Don't you think he could have kept this man from dying?"

At the sealed tomb, Jesus ordered, "Take away the stone." Though he spoke with authority his voice quivered with sadness.

Surely he doesn't mean that? "Lord," I stepped closer to him. "By now there will be a terrible odor. He's been dead four days."

He reminded me, "Didn't I tell you that if you believed you would see God's amazing glory?" *Yes, I believe. Yes, I want to see the glory of God. What does that really mean, though?*

The men nearby listened to our conversation and watched for my cue. I nodded consent.

They shrugged their shoulders and did as I bid. When they rolled away the stone, Jesus lifted his eyes and spoke for everyone to hear, "Father, thank you for hearing me. I know that you always hear me, but I thank you now for the sake of those listening, so that they will believe that you sent me."

I blinked. *He's talking to God as His Father.* It felt strange to hear him speak in such a familiar way. *Of course, Martha, he's the Son of God.*

In a loud voice he commanded, "Lazarus, come out."

"It's my brother!" *This is what Jesus meant by seeing the glory of God!*

My dear brother Lazarus, with hands and feet bound with bandages and his face wrapped in a cloth, stumbled toward us. Every person stood stone still.

Jesus had to wake us up, "Take off his bindings. Let him go."

Mary and I ran to Lazarus, laughing and crying simultaneously. "Lazarus! It's us, your sisters. Let us remove your burial cloths. You were dead and now you are alive."

He stood still as we unwrapped the cloths. He blinked at the bright sunshine. He stared at Mary, then at me. Then he looked behind us to Jesus and smiled, for he knew what happened.

With tears and laughter and songs of joy the dancing crowd closed in on us. Mary and I each took an arm of our brother and led him home. We joined the singing and rejoicing. We have not stopped, for we have seen the glory of God.

Based on the story in John 11:1-44

32 ◆ Compelled

Martha called me rebellious one day, because she found me on a nearby hill staring at the sky instead of working my spinning whorl. Another time, she called me lazy because it took me long to wash our clothing, a job she zipped through. I frustrated her when I stopped to enjoy the birds greet the dawn when I should rush to light the fire. She decided a dreamer like me would never be good at much.

I considered myself serious. I couldn't ignore an internal tug that made me pause to ponder new ideas wherever I happened to be. And maybe that wasn't so bad after all. I remember the time Jesus visited and Martha asked him to reprimand me for listening to him instead of helping her. He told her I made a better choice. I don't see myself better than Martha because of that. I'm thankful it happened because now I'm a little less critical of myself.

That day with Jesus is a good example of how following my heart often leads to trouble. So many times I'm some place where women are not expected. Or even allowed. Like sitting at the men's discussions as they lounged after a meal. Things that feed my soul draw me. I can't help it. I will never forget one such day.

Since Jesus brought our dead brother Lazarus back to life, not a day passed without a song of praise from one or all of us. Our hearts burst with the surety that Jesus was Israel's long-awaited Messiah. And we didn't keep our belief a secret.

Many Judeans were not pleased with the idea that the King of the Jews might be in their midst. They feared he would usurp their power. Some were afraid he was a fraud and people needed protection from him. In our own town of Bethany there were rumblings of a plot to kill him.

With Passover a mere six days away, Jesus and his closest friends stopped in Bethany on the way to Jerusalem. We all worried for his safety.

Martha and I happily served them. When they were visited, Lazarus used every moment to pump Jesus for explanations of Scripture and even of God. That night was no different. As always, Jesus didn't mind the endless questions. In fact, that particular night, his answers became more animated. *He wants to do whatever he can to reach our hearts - to make sure we understand.*

As they lounged and after we cleaned the cups and bowls, their conversation took on a serious note. Or, maybe it was just me because, suddenly, a sense of foreboding flooded through me. *What is this? A feeling of dread? Why?* Still, I could have sat quietly with Martha and paid attention from there. But in spite of myself, I walked to a cupboard where we stored valuable items. *Here it is.*

Quiet as a doe, I carried the pound of spikenard in front of me, as though a gift offering. I moved directly to Jesus. *I must.* Silence fell. No one breathed. I took notice. *I know they're thinking, here she goes again.* But everyone was aware that this time was different, because no one moved to stop me.

I knelt down in front of him, opened the jar, and carefully scooped out a handful of the expensive fragrance. My hands trembled as I slowly and purposefully rubbed the nard into his feet. Tears slipped from my eyes. *Why am I so sad?* In a gesture of honor, I uncovered my hair to fall over his feet. Gently I wiped his feet with my long, thick locks. And then, it was finished. I dropped to the floor and sat counting the frightened beats of my heart.

No one stirred.

Finally, someone coughed. It was Judas Iscariot.

Still no words.

I raised my head. My eyes locked with those of my king.

I guess Judas couldn't bear the spell any longer. Rudely, he interrupted, "Why wasn't this perfume sold? It had to be worth a year's wage. We could have used it to help some poor beggars."

Breaking my gaze, I turned to stare at him. *Oh, my goodness, perhaps he's right. I've been wasteful. There are so many who could benefit. I'll sell what's left and bring the money to the disciples for better use.*

But Jesus brought me back to my intent, "Leave her alone. Let her hold onto this moment. She has prepared my body for burial."

Yes, that is what I'm feeling. It's like, ahead of time, I've participated in his burial. And right now that sad event seems closer than I ever imagined.

And then he added, "You will always have poor people to help. But you won't always have me."

There's pain in my heart. Oh, Jesus, don't remind me of what I already know.

Quietly I slipped across the room to Martha, who embraced me with a tear-drenched face. "You have chosen the better part." I thanked her with a hug.

The evening continued somberly. Judas never spoke another word. At each pause in the subdued conversation, everyone sat in great thought with furrowed brow.

Jesus is my Messiah. I didn't know then what he meant or why I acted as I did, for that matter. I only know now. I also learned that whenever I feel so compelled, I shall act. For it is the King himself who nudges my heart to move.

Based on the story in John 12:1-8

33 ◆ This Year In Jerusalem

O h, yes, it was a night like no other night. And it will forever be engraved in the memory of my heart.

With several other women, I served Jesus and his chosen twelve. For years, we shopped and cooked for them, washed their laundry and mended their clothing as needed. At all times a few of us traveled with them while Jesus taught. To me, it seemed the twelve were in training to spread the good news of true freedom and pure love.

I can speak for the women in our group: we were grateful to serve because we saw the fruit of his teaching through word and example. We learned much and witnessed tremendous change in our own hearts. We became more compassionate, understanding and giving. Serving them was our gift.

Our home, family or business responsibilities determined how much travel each of us could do. We all gave from our own finances. I was the only woman in our group who did not own a profitable business. My husband was a well-paid steward of King Herod. Thankful for my help with the household staff, he shared his wealth generously with me.

The journey with Jesus and his twelve followers was eye-opening. Besides the wisdom of Scripture revealed daily, we saw miracle after miracle as lives changed through words spoken and healings imparted. After the exhausted men retired in the evening, we whispered to one another the wonders observed. We also talked about some of the hard sayings of Jesus.

"Joanna," my friend Susanna whispered to me one night, "What do you think Jesus meant today when he said to that paralytic, 'Your sins are forgiven?'"

"I don't know. I mean, another time he said a person's disease was not because of his sins."

"Right. So I wonder why he felt the need to say that before healing the paralytic?"

I had no better ideas than Susanna. I could only muse, "Maybe healing is about more than the physical needs we see?"

"Maybe," she replied skeptically. "But, also, even though we know he is The Messiah, can he really forgive sins?"

We spent so much time with Jesus and still couldn't grasp his entire picture. Most nights we fell asleep with dozens of questions dancing in our minds. Even so, though unanswered questions rattled through our heads, they were small compared to the immense calm we all experienced.

Whenever we were home, we shared all that we saw and heard. Many of our friends and business associates and, as in my case, household staff, came to believe as we did.

The week before Passover our emotions ran the gamut from high and flying to the depths of dark despair.

It started when Jesus rode into Jerusalem on a donkey and every Jew, it seemed, ushered him in with their cloaks laid out as for a king. They honored him as they waved branches of palm and called out, "Hail, King of the Jews!" I was ecstatic. *We all believe!*

Each day after the first of the week was its own highlight. Intense private instruction to his twelve, healings too numerous to count, stories to the masses that always contained hidden meanings, and constant run-ins with the Pharisees and Sadducees that left us shaking, marked the days.

The very last meal with Jesus arrived. Of course, at that time, none of us knew it was our last with him. And we had no idea how much our understanding of Passover would change, beginning with that night.

Jesus sent two of the men on a mysterious mission to locate a place for us to celebrate. Just like Jesus told them, Peter and John met a man carrying water, one of his Essene friends, I assumed. The man led them, at Peter's request, to an upper room in the city. We were all excited to do our part to prepare for the meal.

An odd feeling swept over us women, and rather than participate in the festival meal as allowed by tradition, we held back while the men reclined for supper, as though it were a typical daily meal. Still, Jesus wanted us to hear everything. As we stood ready to serve, he often glanced our way to make sure we listened.

That night his opening words jolted us. "I can't tell you how much I have wanted to share this Passover meal with you before I go to suffer."

What? Suffer? Instantly my memory was flooded with so many of his hints about how he must suffer and sacrifice for the fulfillment of God's plan. *Oh, no!* But I still had no real idea of the meaning.

"It was a night like no other night," he began with the ancient words of our Fathers.

The atmosphere melted from festive gaiety to somber quiet. Throughout the meal questions thrown to him took precedence over regular conversation. His typical patience shone as he

answered every one. Though there was occasional laughter as someone recalled a shared memory, it was not a party.
Finally, he lifted the last of the unleavened bread. "This is my body which is given for you. Do this in remembrance of me." In a flash I saw that day in Capernaum when he infuriated the Jews with the words, "Anyone who eats this bread will live forever. This is the bread that I give; it is from heaven. It is my flesh that I give for the life of the world." *Is this what he meant?*

The men stole glances at each other. We did, too. The air was thick with silence.

Eventually, the limited conversation picked up again. Until the Cup of Blessing.

Jesus lifted the cup and let his eyes move around the table. He rested them on each person for a split second. And then he looked over at the servants and us.

He gave thanks and then said, "Take this and share it with each other. All of you drink it. This is my Blood of the covenant. It is poured out for the forgiveness of the sins of many. I tell you I shall not drink this wine again from now until that day when I drink the new wine in my Father's kingdom with you."

Those words. I've heard them before. Yes! It was that same day in Capernaum. "Whoever eats my flesh and drinks my blood has eternal life…Whoever eats my flesh and drinks my blood lives and rests securely in me and I live in him." But though I connected the two events, I still couldn't take in their significance.

We looked around the room at each other. Eyes brimmed with understanding, squinted in curiosity, or widened with traces of fear. Even so, they twinkled. Except those of one whose eyes were exceptionally dark.

As the dinner ended, as though on cue, with somber faces we lifted our glasses to toast but we all instinctively changed the words, "<u>This</u> year in Jerusalem!"

That night was so long ago. Yes, His years of ministry changed me. But after that night, and the events that followed, I was completely transformed. Peace and strength planted themselves in my heart and grew like a mighty olive tree that only gets stronger each year, even as part of it dies. Life is not easy, by any means. Yet, I can withstand any storm because I know my life on this earth is only the beginning. And I look forward to that time when I see the light of His face again.

Based on the stories found in Matthew 26:17-29, Mark 14:12-25, and Luke 22:7-38

34 ✦ Love Changed The World

My grandparents used to tell sweet stories of life in the old days. The days of few prejudices when all the residents of our land, regardless of their heritage, enjoyed living side by side. But when Rome declared Cyrene a province, life began to change for our small population of Jews. I needed the break of the Passover Feast before first harvest for many reasons, one being the reminder that I am part of a larger community than we few in Cyrene. I'm always thankful to go.

As our family passed through Jerusalem on our way to my sister's home where we would stay for the feast, we heard wild stories about a man who had been stirring the political pot the last few years. Many times he butted heads with the Pharisees. And he healed people! His activity seemed at a boiling point, evidenced by a procession the day before. People waved palm branches and hailed him as king.

I don't feel good about this. We wove through the noisy city as I wondered. *The very air in Jerusalem seems ready to explode.*

That year my sons traveled with me, which brightened the trip. I've always been proud of Rufus and Alexander. They were hard workers and took their faith seriously. It wouldn't be long before they were kind husbands and good providers. Staying with my sister Esther and her family in Bethany added to my joy. It had been about a year since our families last visited.

In Bethany more outrageous stories about that same man, Jesus of Nazareth, caught our attention. My jaw dropped when Esther told me the craziest account yet. He, literally, called a man out of a tomb. A man who had been dead for at least three days! That man's name was Lazarus.

"Surely that's just a crazy rumor," I shook my head in disbelief.

But my sister's husband knew Lazarus. Esther often visited with his sisters at the market. There was no doubt as to the validity of the story: a man was dead and now lives. *It's almost creepy.*

When Esther and her husband Jacob talked about Jesus, their eyes lit up and their voices rose.

Two evenings before The Feast we sat on the roof talking in hushed tones.

"So what do you really think of this Jesus?" I had to ask.

Jacob and Esther squirmed a bit and looked at each other.

"I can't speak for Esther," Jacob said in a strong, calm voice. "But, I think he's The Messiah that all Israel has waited for."

My eyes widened as I looked into Esther's. "Esther?"

She nodded.

"You both must be kidding." Up went the pitch of my voice. "He's just another zealot claiming to be messiah or, at the least, a magician."

Emphatically they replied in unison, "No."

"How can you be so sure?" I had to know why my educated brother-in-law would take such a position.

"Simon, it's much more than miracles. Though the miracles are great and too numerous to count. The most learned men in the synagogue come to him with questions. His radical ideas do not incite violence, only peace and respect. He's different. Much different from any man any of us has ever known."

Dumbfounded, I tried to absorb the information. I threw my head back and considered the endless gemstones that twinkled in the black night. *What does all this mean?*

Late morning on the day of the celebration I took my boys to Jerusalem. They had never been inside the City of David on the Feast Day. I wanted them to experience the joy of sharing with thousands of people who descended on the holy city from near and far because of our shared faith.

The tension was greater than when we had passed through earlier in the week. *What is going on?*

At a crossroad the tiny streets were lined with residents and pilgrims alike, crushed against each other. Some cried, most jeered.

Oh, no. What did I take my sons to? Are they actually leading a criminal to Golgotha now? I looked at my young sons. Their lips shook without a sound; their eyes were wide as they flattened themselves against me, each clamping a hand.

"What's happening, Father?" the younger son, Rufus, quivered.

"It's a sad event, son. I'm sorry you and your brother are here."

"But what did that man do? Why is he so bloody?" Alexander continued.

"Why is he carrying that big cross?" Rufus wanted to know.

"I'll have to explain when we get back to Esther's." My stomach turned just thinking of that conversation. *Look at him. What did he do? Oh, no, he's stumbling right in front of us. I need to get my boys out of here.*

And just as I leaned in to say, "Come on, boys," a soldier in the procession grabbed my arm.

"You."

I looked up in alarm to a stone-faced, straight-nosed, angry guard.

"You," he repeated. "Carry his cross."

"But, my sons. I can't leave them here alone."

"You heard me," he said, with his left hand on a hip and his right on his sword.

I didn't need a reminder not to refuse a Roman.

I looked at Rufus and Alexander. They shuddered, holding hands, and looked at me with questions in their eyes. "Boys, stay together. Try to follow the procession so I can find you later."

The soldier grabbed my arm again, "Now."

I stepped into the waiting procession and strained to pick up the enormously heavy cross. I looked at the poor prisoner. The skin on his entire bloodied body gaped from a vicious flogging, revealing all his bones. *What a mess they made of him. And why that horrible crown of thorns stuck into his head?*

Step after agonizing step, together we made our way forward. *The guy can barely walk. No wonder he stumbled with this weight.* Sweat already drenched me.

And then women wailed, "Jesus. My Jesus." *Jesus? Esther said this guy could do no wrong. Oh, Esther have you been fooled?*

He stopped and looked at a group of women weighed down with their sorrow, who stretched their hands out to touch him. He spoke, "Daughters of Jerusalem, don't weep for me. If you must mourn, weep for yourselves and your children. Someday soon, everyone will be saying, 'How lucky the women are who don't have any children.'" He continued with a lament.

I didn't want to listen. It all made no sense to me. I tried to sort out what I heard earlier from what I now witnessed.

As we slipped along the slick rocks to the place of the skull I stole a few glances toward the crowd walking with us. *Thank goodness the boys are keeping up.* I saw their little faces poking out from between tunics gathered all around them. My two frightened children, innocent bystanders to the horror of a lifetime, clutched each other tightly. *Oh, my God, have mercy.*

The second they permitted me to set down the cross at Golgotha, I ran to ashen-faced Rufus and Alexander. I knelt and gathered them into my arms. Sobbing, they hid their faces in my shoulders. The sound of iron on iron - nails being hammered - echoed. My eyes roved about the scene. *There are more people here than usual for one of these executions. Maybe it's because of this Jesus. But I can't hang around to find out.*

"Come on, boys," I stood up. "Let's go to Esther's." I held them close to my sides and wove through the crying and jeering crowd.

The vivid memory of that trip has stayed with me all these years. Now I know what happened on that Passover. Now I know who Jesus is. Now I count it an honor and a joy that I carried the cross of the Redeemer of humanity.

That Passover visit to Bethany changed my life forever. And it changed my sons. When Rufus and Alexander grew up, they were leaders of the Jews who recognized Jesus as The Messiah. Life isn't easier. We still live under Roman occupation. And many of us who follow Jesus are persecuted. But we have strength to carry on that we didn't have before that day.

Jesus took something horrifying and made it beautiful all because of love. And Love changed the world.

Based on the stories in Matthew 27:32-44, Mark 15:21-22, and Luke 23:26-33

35 ✦ Changed

Dreidel was my favorite game when I was a little girl. It's a wonder I loved the game, since I could almost never make it spin. The best thing about knowing Jesus then was when he carved me a dreidel with those strong hands that worked carpenter tools like magic. Even the tune he hummed put magic in the air. It was the only dreidel I could ever spin!

Jesus never uttered an unkind word. At least, not in my hearing. The charity I received, he gave to each person he met. He even treated the animals in our village with the same respect he gave people. His deep-set, dark eyes revealed an inner calm that I have never seen in anyone else. And when we were around him, that peace enveloped us all.

He was like a big, protective brother to me while we grew up in Nazareth. I felt special when his muscular arms helped me carry heavy loads. He stood up for me in every argument with my older brothers. It made me feel like I had won, even though he did the work. And if we needed water late in the day, his tall frame, with hand shielding his eyes from the setting sun, stood in the distance, to make sure no robbers or lion lurked to attack me. I felt safe when Jesus was near.

He was brilliant, too. But instead of impressing people with big words and long quotes from Scripture, he laughed as he told stories to explain God's ways. We sat and talked for hours, Jesus and me. He paid attention to every word I spoke, with his eyes locked on mine. In fact, each person he spoke to felt like he was alone in the world with him.

When Aaron and I married, he celebrated with us. When my first child was born, he shared our joy. He was like a brother to us. The day he left Nazareth for his ultimate call, a little ache began in my heart. I didn't understand the feeling. I felt different about my husband whom I love very much. Still, I would have followed Jesus, if circumstances had allowed.

To keep up with his busy new life I asked every traveler to our town if they had news of him. The stories of healings, and teachings, and the times he stood up to the Pharisees amazed me. But not totally. Because I knew Jesus was destined for greatness.

In Jerusalem with my husband for Passover that year, I was glad we stayed in the city, not merely within the prescribed boundaries. I thought we'd have a better chance to see him; it had been such a long time since our last meeting.

Of course, the horrid turn of events blew into my mind and heart like an unexpected sandstorm. Preparation Day was a blur of pain, agony, disbelief and anger. And many tears. I nearly fainted as the crowd chanted to crucify the man who was a brother to me. "He's not a criminal! I yelled to the world. "No! No! No!" I screamed, when I watched the scourging in the praetorium tear and bloody his flesh. I wrung my hands and wailed, when they forced him, battered, bloodied, and beaten, with a crown of thorns pressed into his head, to carry his cross. Just the thought of the Place of the Skull, Golgotha, where he would be executed, made my stomach churn. On the narrow streets I kept pace with the growing crowd, many of whom jeered unfounded accusations and tossed rocks at him. I never left his side, all the way up the hill. Death hung in the air.

My head began to spin with the echo of iron pounding on iron as I watched soldiers bang, bang, bang the huge nails through his hands and feet onto the cross. Then they grabbed hold of the cross and thrust him up with no more care than if he were a butchered lamb. Blood coursed down his face from the long thorns. His gaping flesh was a violation of all that was good. Though I was afraid of potential consequences if I showed my allegiance, I couldn't help but sob. I screamed out my own pain, "Why? Why are you doing this? He never hurt anyone. He is innocent!" No one could hear me over the deafening din of the mass of onlookers that closed in on him.

You can imagine what the next hours were like as they continued to mock and torture such a kind man. Through it all, I could see love and forgiveness in his eyes. And much pain.

Rumors had floated all over Galilee for years about who he was. My heart confirmed the fact long ago. *Why do they want to kill The Messiah?*

I heard his anguish, "My God, my God, why have you forsaken me?" No words can describe the agony on his mother's face as she stood by his blood-soaked body.

A Roman soldier stood near me through the entire spectacle. He didn't actively participate in the wickedness, until he was ordered to hurry the death of my friend by piercing him with a sword. When both water and blood flowed from Jesus' right side, my head jolted around to look at him as he whispered, "Surely this man was the Son of God." *Even Romans believe.*

And then Jesus gasped the words that crushed all hope, "It is done. All is fulfilled. The price is paid. It is finished."

They murdered the Messiah. My heart wrenched. I gasped for air as my body collapsed.

Before another tear could fall after his last words, the sun vanished behind black clouds and the ground broke apart all around us. Fear consumed my sorrow as I tried to stand on the shifting earth, "Help me! Someone help me! Jesus!" *What had they done? What had I done? Could I have been a better friend? What should I have done to prevent this? Oh, my God, forgive me.* Rivers of tears rushed endlessly down my face, while I groped along the ground toward Mary in the midst of chaotic running and crying all around.

Later, when I learned how the veil over the Holy of Holies in the Temple tore in two at the exact moment of his death, wonder began to edge out fear in my heart.

As the earth grumbled and the sky wept ferociously, they removed him from the cross and placed his bloodied body into the arms of his weeping mother. Mary is such a gentle woman. Oh, how she and Joseph loved their only son. As she gently rocked him, letting her tears wash his blood encrusted face, I buried my face in my hands. *I can't watch her pain.*

That night and the next day, I, as many, moved about with glazed eyes, not really seeing. The motions of the Feast were disconnected from my reality. Parched like an old wineskin discarded in the desert, my heart shriveled within.

On the third day, I awoke just before dawn. *What do I hear? The birds are singing!* Only then did I realize that even the birds were mute during the stony silence of the last days. On my mat I listened to a great symphony of delight as every bird and small animal in the land awakened together.

Without disturbing my cousins whom we stayed with, I snuck out and scurried to the house where Mary stayed. I asked if I could join her and the other women to bury my friend properly. We could only hope that wicked Pilate's guards would move the stone for us.

Close to the tomb, the ground shook again. Not like before, but enough to be noticed by everyone. We shared a frightened glance. *Would another earthquake prevent us from giving him the respect and honor he deserved?* The stones and grass were pink with the dawn. Instinctively, as we approached the tomb, my hands shot up to shield my eyes from a bright light. On the ground were the guards. *I think they're dead!* I squinted as we hastened on. *Why is the great stone in front of the tomb moved away?* My heart skipped a beat. *Oh, no. Now what have they done to him?*

All of this happened too fast to track. I no sooner panicked when I saw the guards and the rock, when I realized the blinding light blazed from the stone itself. A figure with a golden face that radiated like lightning, and a shimmery white body, sat on the rock. His brilliance spilled onto the grass and trees and us. I gasped.

"Don't be afraid," he spoke with gentle power that arrested our rising fears. "He isn't here. He has risen, just like he said. Go see for yourselves. And then go quickly to tell his disciples that He will meet them in Galilee."

Our wide eyes blinked at each other. Tears sprang as we rushed to the tomb's entrance and peered inside. And then we fell into each other's arms when we saw the place where they had laid him, empty. Every part of me tingled with awe. Even so, a bit of darkness still threatened my renewed joy.

We turned to run but stopped hard. Before us stood my best friend, my Lord. "Jesus," I whispered as my heart leapt. I dropped to my knees and kissed his feet.

He knew that though we believed, we still were apprehensive. "Don't be afraid," he comforted. "Now, go and tell my brothers that they will see me in Galilee." And in that same instant, He was gone.

"Oh, rejoice in the Lord," we sang with unbridled joy. "Let's hurry to tell his disciples." Our feet fled on wings of angels to tell the Good News that restored all hope; the news that changed our lives and the whole world - forever.

Based on the story in Matthew 28:1-10

36 ✦ A Place For Me

All I am is just another woman in the crowds that followed Jesus, who waited for a miracle, and listened with rapt attention to His simple yet amazing teachings. People like me don't stand out.

Poor Peter. Unlike me, Peter was a well-known Galilean and follower of Jesus, easy to recognize. I stood by when servants approached Peter. He shook his head violently, his eyes grew wide, and he stuttered when they accused him of being a friend of Jesus. Three times he denied that he knew Jesus. When the cock crowed, he let go an anguished wail, convulsed in tears, and staggered away.

I felt his pain, or at least I thought so. And I wondered. *What if it were me they approached? Would I deny knowing him, too? Part of me says, no, of course not. Why would I deny a friend in need?* Even though I was certain Jesus was our long-awaited Messiah, at that moment a tiny seed of doubt in my faith sprouted. *The reality is, I don't know what I would do. I could only hope I would be true.*

You know the horror story of Jesus' violent death. With swollen eyes that stung from too many shed tears, I walked near his mother, all the way up to Golgotha. Disbelief churned in my heavy heart at the turn of events since the week before when people hailed him with palm branches like he was king. By the time he took his last breath, the nagging doubt of faith no longer pricked me.

I was at the well that morning when the women raced down the path. *My goodness, what's going on? Their faces are bathed in light. Their countenance is somehow calm, even as they run.*

Throughout that day the picture of the happy women came to mind often. But when I didn't hear a hint of a rumor, I continued my household chores and tried to deal with the profound sadness that consumed me the previous three days.

As it was, his closest friends kept the secret of his good news to themselves for awhile. Finally, word began to spread. When my neighbor shared the story of his awesome resurrection, chills ran up my arms. Tears splashed down my face, and I grabbed her hands to dance. Soon all of his disciples, myself included, enjoyed that same elation.

Jesus visited his friends where they worked and lived. Funny, I didn't recognize Him at first. But as soon as He broke the bread at our table and gave thanks, a startled breath escaped my lips; in a flash it was as if my eyes opened to His reality.

For forty days after His resurrection, He taught us about His life purpose, and ours. It was a time of delight and overwhelming joy. He ate with us; He laughed and taught. Many people recorded the events; all of the stories spread by word of mouth to towns near and far. Honestly, He performed so many miracles in that time, and imparted so much understanding of Scripture, it can't possibly all be remembered or recorded. We began to see this resurrected Jesus as the valiant, sword-wielding king who would take back Israel. Silly of us. He told us so many times it wouldn't be like that. It wasn't that we didn't believe Him, we just couldn't imagine any other kind of king.

One day He told His closest companions to meet Him at a place called Olivet, a small mountain overlooking Jerusalem. I remember the day vividly. Crystal blue sky, cool air, brilliant white sun. We were full of the wonder of the Lord and sang psalms with gusto as we climbed.

I don't know what the others were thinking. For me, I was grateful for another sweet encounter with our Lord. It never occurred to me we were going there for anything but an inspiring teaching interspersed with laughter, and cloaked in a sense of brotherhood and peace.

"Why do you think He's called us here?" a friend asked as we traveled.

"I think He's going to make a big announcement," a man I didn't know chimed in.

"Like what?" I asked, surprised.

"Like how He will rule the land. And put the Romans in their place once and for all. We finally have a king to deliver us from hundreds of years of bloodshed and occupation."

"No more tyranny," whispered another wistfully.

A few moments after we sat down at the summit, there he was! He appeared suddenly, just as He had been doing so often the past weeks. *How does he do that?* We rushed to the spot where He stood. Excitement hung in the air.

One of those same men asked, "Lord, is this it? Is now the time for you to restore the kingdom of Israel to its former glory?"

We all held our breath. My heart raced.

His measured response stunned us. "That is not for you to know. The Father has laid down epochs and ages by His own authority. But you will be instilled with power when the Holy Spirit arrives and envelops you. And you will testify about me in Jerusalem and throughout all Judea and Samaria and even to the ends of earth." *What does He mean?*

He raised his hands and blessed us. The sky broke open and a shimmery white cloud came down.

I blinked and rubbed my eyes. *I'm seeing things. I shouldn't have been looking into the bright sun.*

But, no, it was true. A brilliant cloud did envelop Jesus and then – hard as this is to imagine – it lifted him away farther than we could see, right before our eyes.

"He's gone!" many of us shouted together.

"Where is he?" others asked as we continued to gaze into the cloudless turquoise canopy.

In the same way Jesus had appeared since his resurrection, two men nobody knew suddenly stood in the exact spot where Jesus had been.

"Men and women of Galilee," their unison baritone voices penetrated my mind. "Why are you standing around looking at the sky? Jesus has been received into heaven. He will come the same way you watched him go."

Wide-eyed and silent, we glanced around at each other. And when I looked back to ask these strangers to explain, they were gone!

Words spilled from me, "Do you remember when he said he will go and prepare a place for us? This is it! He's gone ahead of us!"

We leapt into each other's arms. We jumped and raised our arms toward heaven. We yelled. We cried and we laughed. With joy that will never be contained we sang all the way back to Jerusalem, "Blessed is he who comes in the name of the Lord!" We still didn't understand everything but we believed – a simple act of faith.

Dayenu - it would have been enough - for him to rise from the dead and ascend before our eyes. But we gathered in Jerusalem, and waited just as he told us to. We didn't know how long we'd have to wait. We didn't even know what to expect. We trusted Him that at the right time we would grasp what was happening. When the Holy Spirit descended to infuse us with pure joy and wisdom, He also filled us with total understanding. *The Son of the Living God is the King of kings. His kingdom is not like any kingdom of this earth and it will have no end. He does not rule by force. His kingdom is one of peace and dignity for all mankind. This is Jesus. He has fulfilled the law and the prophets, just as he said!*

Our lives were forever changed. The world is forever changed as we followed His instructions and spread out to the ends of the earth. Wherever we are, we proclaim the Good News and perform mighty works in His name.

Based on the stories in Mark 16:19, Luke 24:36-52, and Acts 1:1 - 2:13

Commonly Known Bible Stories by Chapter

Chapter Title/Commonly Known Bible Story/Scripture Reference

References

Boyle, Isaac. *The Ecclesiastical History of Eusebius Pamphilus, Bishop of Cesarea in Palestine*. Grand Rapids, MI: Baker Book House, 1990. Print.

Brown, Raphael. *The Life of Mary as Seen by the Mystics*. Charlotte, NC: TAN, 1951. Print.

Edersheim, Alfred. *Sketches of Jewish Social Life*. Print.

Healy, Mary. *The Gospel of Mark*. Grand Rapids, MI: Baker Academic Baker Group, 2008. Print.

O'Brian, Patrick. *Daily Life in the Time of Jesus*. New York, NY: Hawthorne, 1962. Print.

Packer, J.I., M. C. Tenney, and W. White, Jr., eds. *The Bible Almanac*. 2nd ed. Thomas Nelson, 1980. Print.

Voobus, Arthur. *History of Asceticism in the Syrian Orient, A Contribution to the History of Culture in the near East*. Waversebaan 49: Louvain, 1958. Print.

Whiston, William. *The Works of Josephus, Complete and Unabridged*. 4th ed. Peabody, MA: Hendrickson, 1989. Print.

Wieand, Albert Cassel. *A New Harmony of the Gospels*. 2nd ed. Grand Rapids, MI: Wm B Eerdmans, 1950. Print.

Wills, Ed. *Where Do I Go From Here? A Guidebook for Life's Transitions*. © 2013 by William Edward Wills. Print.

Numerous internet sources including, but not limited to:

12ApostlesoftheCatholicChurch.com

AncientHistory.about.com

AngieAway.com

Archive.Archeology.org

Bible.ca

BibleAtlas.org

BiblePlaces.com

BibleStudyManuals.net

BibleWalks.com
Blessit.com
Blogs.Aljazeera.com/Syria Live Blog
Catholic.com
ChristusRex.org
FishingTheAbyss.com
Hoshanarabbah.org
JerusalemPerspective.com
JesusCentral.com
NPR.org
TaylorMarshall.com

About Cheryl Ann Wills

Cheryl Ann Wills is an author and entrepreneur. From childhood through college and the workplace, she has been a writer. Her writing varies from non-fiction to children's stories. This is her first published work of historical fiction.

Her passion is to give back to society by making a difference. This she does through writing what she hopes will open hearts to life-changing ideas, by teaching children to read to increase their future value to themselves and society, and by teaching people how wise health choices can be foundational to fulfilling our destiny.

She and her husband, Ed, have three fabulous daughters and two happy dogs. Family time, photography and painting, cycling, and hiking help her maintain balance in life. Daily prayer and meditation keep Cheryl centered.

You can visit her at CherylAnnWills.com

Made in the USA
Columbia, SC
14 March 2019